The Middle School—And Beyond

Paul S. George
Chris Stevenson
Julia Thomason
James Beane

Association for Supervision
and Curriculum Development
Alexandria, Virginia

Association for Supervision and Curriculum Development
1250 N. Pitt Street • Alexandria, Virginia 22314-1403
Telephone (703) 549-9110   FAX (703) 549-3891

Printed in the United States of America by Banta Company.

Ronald S. Brandt, *ASCD Executive Editor*
Nancy Modrak, *Managing Editor, Books*
Julie Houtz, *Senior Associate Editor*
Carolyn Pool, *Associate Editor*
Cole Tucker, *Editorial Assistant*
Gary Bloom, *Manager, Design and Production Services*
Stephanie Kenworthy, *Assistant Manager, Production Services*
Valerie Sprague, *Desktop Specialist*
Karen Monaco *(Cover Design), Graphic Designer*

$14.95
ASCD Stock No. 611-92016
ISBN: 0-87120-190-9

Library of Congress Cataloging-in-Publication Data

The Middle school—and beyond / Paul S. George . . . [et al.].
        p.   cm.
    Includes bibliographical references (p.   ).
    ISBN 0-87120-190-9 : $14.95
    1. Middle schools—United States.   2. School management and
organization—United States.   I. George, Paul S.   II. Association
for Supervision and Curriculum Development.
    LB1623.5.M53   1992
    373.2'36—dc20   92-3662
                                                              CIP

The Middle School— And Beyond

Foreword

Suppose, this fall, that your school district were to move all of the 9th graders into the high school building and do away with the traditional junior high. Suppose, in the old junior high building, a "new" school were created especially for 6th, 7th, and 8th graders.

Imagine, in this new configuration, that all of the teachers were tuned in to the developmental needs of their students, that all the teachers preferred to work at the middle level, and that all the teachers had received special training to help them better communicate with and reach out to their students. Imagine a group of students who discovered that their teachers respected them, had a sense of humor and fair play, cared about their lives outside the classroom, and sought their active involvement in such a variety of projects that no one had to feel left out, alienated, or "different."

Imagine, too, that these teachers and students were encouraged to work cooperatively together on interdisciplinary, even multi-age, teams; that teachers and students, regardless of age and background, found that they enjoyed being together and creating experiences inside and out of the school building that were meaningful to the students and made them feel secure, confident, and committed to their own education.

What if, far from happening some day in the future, all of this had already happened in many districts over many years?

In fact, this student-responsive school, the heart of the middle school movement, has been around for decades. Although it is indeed still new in many places, the middle school concept has been adopted and accepted in districts across the country for a variety of reasons: as a tool for desegregation, to cope with changing demographics and exploding enrollments, to meet state funding requirements. But the resurging middle school movement of the '90s offers the best rationale yet: to address the special learning needs of students at a crucial stage in their development as they prepare for a vision of a future that has never been faster changing.

The numerous vignettes that Paul George and his associates offer in this book attest to a middle school movement ("one of the most important stories of this century," according to the authors) that provides our students with a strong academic program, untold opportunities for success, and a caring environment. In middle schools across the United States, adults are actively participating in youngsters' lives, students are constructing their own knowledge, schools are committed to and deeply involved in community life, and teachers are cooperatively creating the kinds of learning experiences that breed excellence.

Beyond their own walls, middle schools are having a profound effect on the entire range of American schooling, K-12. The middle schools' emphasis on the characteristics and interests of students, the importance of a close-knit school community, the accommodation of diversity, and the integration of the curriculum has found its way to many elementary and secondary schools as well.

The Middle School—And Beyond comes to ASCD members in the midst of transforming learning. It offers all of us inspiration for continuing our examination of paradigms, practices, and new possibilities. And it reinforces our commitment to making change happen now.

CORRINE HILL
ASCD President
1991-92

1

Toward the Middle School

In the 1940s and '50s, comic books were the rage among young adolescents. They ranged from "Superman" and "Tales from the Crypt!" to "Mad Magazine." Any American who was a kid back then can probably remember with fondness a comic book of some kind.

What might not come so readily to mind is a particular advertisement that appeared on the back of virtually every issue of many of these comic books for several years. It featured a beautiful young girl lying on a blanket at the beach. Beside her was a rather emaciated young man who came to be known to millions of comic book readers as the "98-pound weakling." In the next frame, a muscular bully arrives on the scene and performs what we might have called, back then, a dastardly deed. He kicks sand in the face of the 98-pound weakling! The thin young man is humiliated and the pretty young girl so embarrassed that she walks off with the bully, leaving the weakling an emotional wreck as well.

Fortunately for truth, justice, and the American way, in the next frame of the advertisement the "world's most perfectly formed human being" appears on the beach beside the 98-pound weakling. Charles Atlas! Charles Atlas teaches the young man the secret of strength, confidence, health, success, and vitality. In a short time, as time passes in the comic books at least, the weakling is transformed into a figure of muscular and mental virility.

Back on the beach for the final scenes, the newly rebuilt and now deservedly confident young man gives the bully a well-deserved shot to the jaw and regains the esteem and the company of the pretty young blonde. All is well and right with the world.

In the final frame, Charles Atlas volunteers to teach us the secret! For the paltry sum of $2.00, we could learn the secret by which the 98-pound weakling was transformed. Millions of American adolescents (including two of the authors) mailed in the money and were delivered the secret. Some of us practiced for weeks and months. Most of us, we suspect, gave up after a few sessions in front of the mirror. Although we might not have developed the kind of biceps that Charles Atlas had, a generation has had his secret deeply etched in the back of its minds.

What was the secret that Charles Atlas taught? And why is it in any way important to American education?

The name of Charles Atlas' secret was "Dynamic Tension!!" Dynamic tension. Actually, there was something to it. The modern practice of isometrics—growth resulting from the careful balancing of opposing muscle groups—was foreseen by yesterday's version of Arnold Schwartzenegger.

In some ways, more seriously, this is what the middle school movement and this book are both about: an educational version of dynamic tension. Successful middle level education, we believe, is most often the result of just such a careful balance. High-quality middle schools result from the creative balance between elementary and secondary perspectives, between specialization and generalization, between curriculum and community, between equity and excellence, between teaching the mind and touching the heart. Dynamic tension, in one way or another, has always been a part of middle level education.

Both the history and the current status of middle level education in America are the result of a type of dynamic tension, a struggle between a philosophical commitment to improving programs for young adolescents, on the one hand, and the demands of expediency on the other. These two factors, constant throughout the last century, have created the middle level education of today. We believe that these two factors will continue to influence the development of middle level education in the future, and that contemporary middle level educators should be cognizant of them.

■ ■ ■

Origins of the Junior High School

More than a century ago, educators began to perceive an imbalance in the continuum of education. In 1872, concern over the average age of entering freshmen at Harvard prompted Charles W. Eliot, president of the college, to initiate an investigation of ways to improve and reduce the total program of elementary and secondary education prior to college admission. He pursued this issue throughout his chairmanship of the famous Committee of Ten on Secondary School Studies.

The Committee of Ten recommended, in 1893, that the secondary school program should begin two grades earlier, with six years of elementary and six years of secondary education. This issue of correct balance (or tension) between elementary and secondary styles of education became the subject of discussion for the next twenty years. Eventually, the Committee on Economy of Time in Education, reporting in 1913, made the first specific mention of a separate junior division of secondary education. In the years to come, school districts all over the nation experimented with either a 6-6 or 6-3-3 programmatic division of the schools (Gruhn and Douglas 1971).

Plans for the first junior high schools contained components that would be very familiar to today's middle school educator. The school was to be based on the characteristics of young adolescents and concerned with all aspects of growth and development. It would be a school designed to provide continued work in learning skills while bringing more depth to the curriculum than had been the case in the elementary schools. It would emphasize guidance and exploration, independence and responsibility. The junior high school would provide the final portion of general education and offer a transition to the high school years (Tye 1985). None of this should sound strange to contemporary educators; surprising, perhaps, but not strange.

Even at the time the earliest junior high schools were established, however, there were factors, other than ideas about what would constitute the most effective program, that significantly influenced the design of the system. In many less populated states, for example, the junior high school became a substitute for the high school. That is, if a particular community had a small enrollment of students of high school age, then they were likely to be designated as a junior high school district, and the few students who did go on to high school had to do so at the county seat, where sufficient student enrollment could be assembled (A.O. White, personal communication, February 1989).

The "preparation for preparation" syndrome had begun. Having been influenced by and shaped in an imitation of European models of university education, Harvard reciprocated by influencing, in turn, most of the private and public universities in America. Indeed, many would argue that staff members of virtually all American universities still strive daily to shape their college or university to be as much like the Harvard model as possible. Some have even taken pride in being known as the Harvard of the South, or of the West.

These same universities, in states across the nation, exerted a similar influence on the high schools of those states. Preparation for university study was the raison d'etre of the American high school until the middle of the 20th century. Many might argue that this is still the preferred and most influential function of the high school.

In turn, all too often, it appears that in most states and many school districts the junior high school began to take on the characteristics and components of the high school to which a few select students would be sent. This choice was made over the option of focusing on the appropriate education for all young adolescents. With the school district staff reasoning that it would be important to have a program that was connected securely to the high school, the junior high school, also having originated as a secondary school, became more and more a high school replica.

By the middle of the 20th century, following World War II, the junior high school reached the height of its popularity, in terms of numbers. Dramatic growth occurred. The number of junior highs soared from a few hundred in the first two decades of the century to well over 5,000 by 1960 (Howard and Stoumbis 1970). By that same year, 80 percent of America's high school graduates had gone through an elementary-junior-senior high school organization (Alexander and McEwin 1989b). The influence of higher education, the need to deal with growing masses of immigrants, and burgeoning school enrollments following the two world wars all contributed to the increasing number of junior high schools (Lounsbury 1960).

At the same time, programmatically, many a junior high school steadily became more and more a little high school in virtually every way. Teachers were organized in academic departments (as they were in the high schools and the universities and at Harvard), rather than in the interdisciplinary core curriculum groups that the literature of the junior high school recommended. Students were promoted or retained on a subject-by-subject basis. Elective programs focused on specialization that would lead to quasi-majors at the high school rather than the exploration envisioned by other early junior high school educators. Rigid grouping patterns based on perceived ability (measured by I.Q.) or prior achievement became characteristic of the junior high school in many districts. To their dismay, teachers who had prepared for high school teaching often ended up by default in the junior high school. Too many administrators saw their assignment to the junior high as a way station, an intermediate step to their real aspiration, which was the senior high school (where they had been an assistant principal) and beyond. The junior high school, in practice, was shaped by the high school, by the state university, by Harvard, and by European universities established five centuries earlier.

As the structure of modern American society grew more and more flexible, more complex, more urban, and more pluralistic, the stresses on all levels of education increased. The conflict between the ideal and the real in the American junior high school stood out most glaringly. The inadequacies of many junior high schools became more and more obvious. Both liberal and conservative philosophical positions described the mid-century junior high school in critical terms. Reform became increasingly urgent.

Reforming the Junior High

In 1961, ASCD published *The Junior High School We Need* (Grantes et al. 1961). The authors pointed out that the contemporary junior high school was a hybrid institution, a school with an identity crisis as severe as the identity crisis endured by many of the young students within it. While the 7th and 8th grades retained some semblance of the elementary school, the 9th grade was influenced most strongly by the high school. This was especially so because the credit-counting process for high school graduation always had and continued to include the 9th grade. The high school, in fact, never truly relinquished control of this grade; the 9th grade was a high school year, simply housed in a different building.

The 1961 ASCD report continued to describe the ideal junior high school in terms that were very different from actual practice. The document's authors, Grantes, Noyce, Patterson, and Robertson, identified the best contemporary junior high schools as characterized by, among other things, moderate size; block-of-time instruction; flexible scheduling; teachers prepared for and devoted to teaching young adolescents; and modern instructional techniques.

They predicted that the junior high school of the future would be "ungraded" in the sense of permitting student groupings to be designed without reference to chronological number of years in school; without bells; rich in guidance services; and characterized by differential assignments for teachers. The new junior high school would make use of modern developments in technology (no mention of computers yet) and would have "the development of democratic values as its central commitment" (Grantes et al. 1961, p. 19).

The new junior high school never materialized. Instead, the emerging middle school began to take its place. Prior to the publication of the 1961 document, schools that were called "middle schools" were opening in more than a few districts around the country. Among the first were Upper St. Clair, Pennsylvania; Centerville, Ohio; Barrington, Illinois; Mt. Kisco, New York; and Saginaw, Michigan. By 1965, a quarter of a century ago, William Alexander and others were calling for a new school in the middle, one that would utilize a different organizational pattern (5 or 6 through 8) to achieve the century-old purposes of middle level education. Without the 9th grade, these new schools would be less controlled by the high school and freer to adapt to the real needs of older children and young adolescents (Alexander and Williams 1965).

Middle Schools Emerge

A decade later, following the publication of a number of influential textbooks and journal articles and in recognition of the growing number of middle schools, ASCD established a Working Group on the Middle School and the Early Adolescent Learner. The group's subsequent report, *The Middle School We Need* (ASCD 1975), reemphasized the developmental characteristics of young adolescents and the need to respond to those characteristics in appropriate educational ways. As had the earlier publication in 1961, however, this report pointed to the variance between accepted models for early adolescent education and the actual implementation of those models in any significant number of schools.

There appeared to be great similarity between the pedagogical vision of the aging junior high school and that of the newborn middle school. Unfortunately, there was a similar absence of a vision for the actual day-to-day practices in either older junior high schools or newer middle schools. The Council authors wrote: "The available research indicates a significant gap between the main tenets of the theoretical middle school concept proposed by leading middle school authorities and actual educational practices in most middle schools" (ASCD 1975, p. 3).

Glaring discrepancies between the ideals and the practices of the junior high and the middle school grew out of the continuing tension between an educational vision and the expediencies of everyday life in

American school districts. Programs of both the junior high school and the middle school have suffered from other nonpedagogical, but nonetheless critically important, factors impinging on education. In the case of the junior high school, the influence of the secondary school and university, as well as the confusion of the name, brought about a proliferation of such schools with the name (junior high) and grade organization, but with little implementation of the programmatic goals of the junior high.

The middle school, during the first twenty-five years of its existence, has suffered from a similar burden. Many, indeed a majority, of the first middle schools may have been opened for reasons having very little to do, directly, with the characteristics and needs of young adolescents. Until recently, this fact has been the cause of more than a little skepticism and cynicism counterbalancing the claims, pronouncements, and hopes of middle school advocates.

One of the social forces that contributed to the great increase in the number of middle schools in the 1960s and '70s and even later was the movement toward racial desegregation of the schools. In district after district, particularly but not exclusively in the South, central office leaders discovered that reorganizing to a middle school format would significantly increase the amount of school desegregation. A school district, especially one faced with a court order to desegregate, would submit a plan to close several junior high schools and move the 9th graders on to the high school. Then the 6th and sometimes the 5th graders would be moved into newly created middle schools. These students, having attended sharply segregated neighborhood elementary schools in the past, were now bussed, often some distance, to the new, much more desegregated middle schools. This process, combined with other desegregation guidelines, could result in a far more desegregated school district and was met with approval in many federal courts. It is possible that hundreds of middle schools were created to achieve this important and urgent social goal.

Unfortunately, almost all of the attention of school district planners, and many of the resources, went to the accomplishment of the primary goal, desegregating the schools, by moving children from one school to another. The change in grade-level attendance patterns was often fairly expedient. All too frequently, the move was not accompanied by carefully planned, long-lived programmatic changes in the new middle schools. Even in districts that attempted to implement the whole middle school concept, program planners knew painfully little about the concept or the difficulties inherent in implementing such fundamental changes in the way students and teachers are organized to learn and teach. Consequently, far too many of the new schools were middle schools solely in name and grade level.

During the same decades, demographic patterns also exerted a substantial effect on the number of new middle schools. Throughout major portions of the United States (especially in well-established areas in the East and the Midwest), pupil enrollment patterns sharply reversed themselves, and districts that had experienced skyrocketing enrollments in the two decades after World War II now found themselves experiencing just the opposite. Enrollments in many districts plummeted to the point that "riffing"—for reduction in force—became a new household term. Hundreds of school districts faced sizable layoffs of career teachers and the unpleasant prospect of closing schools that were centers of community tradition and values. Many a school board election was won or lost on the question of closing high schools.

Simultaneously, however, a so-called baby boomlet was responsible for a large group of children entering the elementary schools. This, along with the advent of kindergarten, caused enrollment in the early elementary grades to swell to the bursting point at the same time the hallways of many high schools echoed with the sound of far fewer adolescent footsteps. Dozens and dozens of school districts were faced with the prospect of opening new elementary schools at the same time they were closing high schools.

At some point in the process, and probably somewhere in the demographically hard-pressed Midwest, astute central office planners must have discovered that the implementation of middle schools might solve the problems brought on by closing high schools. They could close the junior high schools, instead, and move the 9th graders to the high schools, thus resulting in a 25 percent overnight increase in high school enrollment. The school board would not have to vote to close good old "Central High."

Concurrently, the 6th graders could be moved out of the elementary schools into the new middle schools, thus creating 20 percent more room in those elementary buildings and making it unnecessary to build a new elementary school. Little wonder that this solution was found to be exceedingly palatable for a decade or so by many central office administrators and school board members eager to do the right thing, and to avoid so-called career-limiting decisions for themselves. As with many middle schools that were created to speed racial desegregation, a multitude of schools emerging from the need to satisfy changing demographic patterns became middle schools only in name and grade level.

More recently, a new wave of middle schools has swept forth as a result of the national attention on education during the '80s and the comprehensive state legislation that accompanied a raft of critical reports. Virtually every state enacted legislation designed to strengthen high school academic programs as a result of *A Nation at Risk* (Gardner 1983). As usual, improvements contemplated for the high school have had serious repercussions at the middle level.

Most often, school districts responded to the cry for excellence in the high schools by imposing stricter standards and increased graduation requirements. In many states, this meant that the placement of the 9th grade in the junior high school became glaringly inadequate. So, in order to comply with the requirements of new state legislation and to do so in the manner most likely to secure maximum state funding, district after district found it expedient to physically move the 9th grade into the high school building. Voila! New middle schools.

By the late 1980s, however, many educators' experiences with the middle school had become increasingly positive. School district staff members, teachers, and patrons were discovering that, properly organized and operated, middle schools often delivered substantial improvements for the district (George and Oldaker 1985a, 1985b). These positive experiences, we believe, have influenced a substantial number of school districts to implement exemplary middle schools, even though their initial goal wasn't to create schools responsive to the characteristics and needs of young adolescent learners.

These positive experiences have in turn led school district leaders to explore the middle school concept for its benefits, apart from any other exigencies. Now, whole states have endorsed the middle school concept and are encouraging their districts to move toward middle schools. The California State Department of Education has published a task force report, *Caught in the Middle* (Middle Grade Task Force 1987), giving strong encouragement to reorganization. Florida has implemented legislation (Speaker's Task Force 1984) favoring middle schools and interdisciplinary teams, and funding the process with enhancement grants for more than $30 million annually. Georgia has made similar moves. Others, like New York, appear to be taking similar steps. Small wonder that school districts that previously had little motivation to move to middle schools are now seriously considering it.

An increasingly clear and firm national consensus has emerged about characteristics of the most effective middle level schools. The National Middle School Association, at its 1988 annual conference, adopted several resolutions highlighting this professional agreement (NMSA Resolutions Committee 1989). The resolutions reasserted the uniqueness of a middle level program focusing on the characteristics and needs of young adolescents, affirmed the interdisciplinary team organization as the most appropriate arrangement for middle level teachers and students, urged the preservation of exploration in the curriculum, and condemned common tracking and rigid ability grouping. These resolutions clearly affirm the traditional concepts favored by leaders in the middle grades for the last century.

At approximately the same time that NMSA's resolutions were adopted, the National Association of Secondary School Principals issued *An Agenda for Excellence at the Middle Level* (NASSP 1985). This document advocated schools' adapting to students' developmental needs by including student advisement programs and variety in instructional strategies. NASSP envisioned schools "organized around teaching teams that plan for and work with a clearly identified group of students, thereby assuring that every student is well-known by a group of teachers" (p. 10), and teacher and administrator education specifically designed for middle level schools. Clearly, these recommendations are congruent with those of the National Middle School Association, thus signalling a widespread acceptance of the middle school concept.

While the pace at which the junior high-middle school reorganization is occurring must eventually slow, middle school education will continue to be the concept guiding the education of young adolescents in America for decades to come. In the twenty-year period from 1970 to 1990, the total number of traditional junior high schools (grades 7-9) declined by about 53 percent while the total number of middle schools (grades 5 or 6 through 8) increased by over 200 percent (Alexander and McEwin 1989b). In some states, it is possible that the junior high school, as a grade-level entity, will completely disappear by the end of the century.

Consensus on the Critical Elements of the Middle School

The important question, then, is not whether the middle school will be the predominant organizational pattern. It already is. At issue is whether such schools will be operated in a manner designed to respond directly to the characteristics and needs of young adolescents. Will the educational experience of early adolescence be different, or will the names and grade levels of the schools have changed while the programs remain the same? Fortunately, all evidence suggests that substantial changes have also begun to occur in the very nature of how the middle school program is organized and operated.

Alexander and McEwin (1989a), in a major national survey, found that important changes in middle school organization and curriculum have accompanied the dramatic increase in numbers. For example, interdisciplinary team organization has increased tremendously in the last twenty years. Whereas in 1968 fewer than 10 percent of the schools reported interdisciplinary team organization, in 1988 approximately one-third did so. In 1988, nearly 400 reported having advisor-advisee programs, while the likelihood of these programs being in place in 1968 was so slight that the question wasn't even asked.

In addition, many school leaders now report a rationale for middle school implementation responding to the characteristics and needs of early adolescence, rather than reflecting administrative expediency. They also report an earlier and broader range of interest-exploratory courses and activities. Alexander and McEwin's survey clearly indicates that the middle school program is expanding rapidly, albeit not as rapidly as the number of schools. They conclude:

> The middle level is moving toward becoming a full partner in the new three-level system of education below the college level. Much progress has been made in the implementation of desirable characteristics by many middle level schools. The majority on most characteristics, however, have yet to provide features they need, and probably wish to have. We suspect that most schools at all levels have a few such gaps between desired and actual characteristics, and hope that such data as reported here for the middle level will help school leaders and supporters to improve education at every level (Alexander and McEwin 1989b, p. 44).

Simultaneously, Gordon Cawelti (1988) conducted a parallel national survey for ASCD, utilizing a carefully selected sample. The Cawelti study confirmed the findings of Alexander and McEwin. Cawelti concluded:

> The middle school organization of grades 6-8 is most likely to provide the key characteristics or program features commonly advocated as most appropriate to the needs of students aged 10-14 (p. 1). . . . and middle schools are much more likely to use a teacher-advisor program, provide transition and articulation activities, use interdisciplinary teaching and block schedules, and provide staff development activities that extend the range of teaching strategies appropriate to their students (p. 4).

Shortly after the appearance of these two research studies, the Carnegie Council on Adolescent Development presented the findings of its Task Force on Education of Young Adolescents. In *Turning Points: Preparing Youth for the 21st Century* (1989), the task force made a number of recommendations that powerfully reinforce the directions in which both the Alexander and McEwin study and the ASCD study indicated middle level education had been moving. Perhaps because of the public prestige associated with the members of the commission, and because of the quality of work previously completed by other Carnegie groups, *Turning Points* has received a great deal more public attention than either of the other two studies.

As is too often the case, the headlines associated with the report's release seriously misrepresented its contents. On the day it was released, headlines in newspapers around the country read "Middle Schools Fail the Nation's Youth." In fact, the recommendations of the report were exactly the opposite. Instead of an indictment of the middle school concept, the report was an almost complete and enthusiastic endorsement of that perspective. Totally rejecting the traditional, heavily secondary approach, the Carnegie group placed its recommendations squarely in line with what middle school educators had been saying for years.

The Carnegie report urged schools to provide young adolescents with:

1. *Small communities for learning within the larger school buildings.* In its first recommendation, the commission urged schools to create "smallness within bigness," a concept that has been an important aspect of the middle school lexicon for decades.

2. *A core academic program for all learners.* The commission spelled out a very general set of curriculum goals similar to programs advocated by many middle school educators.

3. *Success experiences for all students.* The commission urged the elimination of tracking and between-class ability grouping, promotion of cooperative learning, and other experiences likely to broaden the range of students experiencing success in the average middle school.

4. *Empowerment for teachers and administrators in making decisions about the experiences of middle grades students.* The organization of schools into academic teams and shared decision making are central components of the middle school concept; the research indicates that middle schools have been moving in this direction for the last twenty years and that 6-8 middle schools are much more likely to employ these practices than the 7-9 junior high school.

5. *Teachers who are expert at teaching young adolescents.* The attempt to develop programs to prepare and certify such teachers has been at the top of the middle school agenda.

6. *Improved academic performance fostered through health and fitness.* Here the commission moved out in front of typical middle school practices, although not out of line with typical middle school philosophy.

Some would argue, however, that health and fitness are laudable goals in themselves and do not need to be attached to academic performance for their justification.

7. *Families reengaged in the education of young adolescents.* The commission recommended giving families meaningful roles in school governance and other concepts that are not currently the vogue in American middle schools, but which would find support among middle school educators.

8. *Schools that are reconnected with their communities.* The group recommended service projects, partnerships, and other collaborative efforts that would enhance any middle school program.

Further evidence of what some might call the maturation of the middle school movement is contained in a national survey conducted by the Effective Middle Grades Program at the Johns Hopkins University Center for Research on Elementary and Middle Schools (CREMS), and presented in a special section of the *Kappan* (Epstein 1990). Once again, the data appear to indicate that more and more middle level schools have, or are planning to, adopt practices that are responsive to the needs of young adolescents.

Grade span and trends in middle grades practices are definitely linked, says the Johns Hopkins research team, although it is the practices and not the grade levels that really count. They conclude that practices long deemed to be important by middle school educators (e.g., advisory programs, interdisciplinary team organization, and school transition programs) are supported by "good evidence that strong implementation yields benefits that are educationally significant" (MacIver 1990). Principals of schools dedicated to early adolescence predict that they will increasingly adopt flexible scheduling, more exploratory courses and mini-courses, the use of interdisciplinary teams (with common planning periods), parent involvement, advisory programs, cooperative learning, and variations of long-term teacher-student relationships (Epstein 1990). These trends appear to blend perfectly with those identified in other studies.

It is rare, indeed, that four major, carefully conducted, national studies focus simultaneously on a similar concern, as has happened in the case of contemporary middle school education. It is as comforting as it is rare to learn how much support each study lends to the others. We can, as a profession, be fairly certain that significant changes have occurred in the grade organization of middle level education in America. Even more, we can be encouraged by the knowledge that, in spite of the circumstances surrounding its birth and adolescence, the middle school is maturing beautifully; and that one sign of this maturation is the nation's increasing readiness to think of middle schools as a legitimately separate and distinct phase of education in America.

We believe, of course, that much remains to be accomplished. It is true, as the Johns Hopkins study and the Cawelti and Alexander and McEwin studies indicate, that the majority of schools in the middle remain, programmatically, far from achieving the goals of the Carnegie recommendations. And, as Alexander and McEwin point out, the potential for the middle school concept to contribute to the improvement of education at every level is largely unfulfilled. Our purpose, in this book, is to contribute to both these worthy ends. We seek the further implementation of the middle school concept in all middle level schools. We advocate for all schools, K-12, implementing appropriate practices emerging from nearly three decades of being shaped and strengthened in the heat of the contemporary American educational blast furnace.

We believe that these two goals—the continued implementation of the middle school concept and the use of appropriate components across the K-12 educational spectrum—can best be furthered by attention to fundamental and central concerns in middle school education. Those concerns are the topics of the rest of this book.

2

Teachers and Students: Relationships and Results

Charles Adams (1989), recently retired after teaching for fifteen years in Fayetteville, Arkansas, talked about Maggie, a 6th grader with extremely poor reading skills. He had tried several ways to help her, but without success. One day, in a conference with her mother, he found out that Maggie liked to cook and sew but was frustrated by her inability to read recipes and sewing patterns. Adams had his hook. Beginning with a list of cooking and sewing vocabulary words, he explained to her that if she could learn these words, she could use them for the rest of her life. It worked. Soon Maggie was able to bake Adams' favorite banana cake, which she proudly brought to school to share with the class. Adams learned something very important in working with Maggie. He says he learned "never to stop trying to find something a child has interest in and using that interest to motivate the child" (p. 58).

■   ■   ■

The Importance of Relationships

Many of us who chose a career in education possess cherished memories of teachers who influenced us as we were growing up. Some of us may have been affected by these teachers in our own decisions to become educators. And some of us may even call these teachers to mind today as we make professional decisions, imagining how they would have handled the one issue or another. Who knows how long we carry within us the values and character of teachers who met and meet our needs so well?

In 1986, astronaut Margaret Lathlan was a keynote speaker at the annual conference of the National Middle School Association. In her address at the opening general session, she talked about how much she treasured the influence of her teachers; and she shared stories that conveyed their personal integrity, maturity, and good humor. Then she invited everyone in the audience who had been influenced by their teachers to utter those teachers' names aloud. A prolonged reverberating rumble through the hall testified to the audience's accord.

At the beginning of each semester, we ask our teacher education students to identify the most significant influence in their schooling when they were emerging adolescents. Overwhelmingly, they cite their teachers. And, fortunately, most of their memories are happy. Like Margaret Lathlan and her audience, our students are aware and deeply appreciative of how much their teachers have meant to them. Less frequently, but often enough, our students also have bitter memories to share—memories of teachers who were uncaring and even cruel and malicious, who caused them to feel embarrassment or humiliation in front of their peers.

As important as understanding students' needs, it is necessary to understand teachers' needs and how they can be addressed in school. A popular stereotype is that teachers wind up teaching at the middle level because they've been unsuccessful at getting appointed to a high school position and can't do anything else. Why do they endure such ignominy? What's in it for them? To explore these questions we'll draw from teachers' writing and comments in informal interviews.

What Do Students Need in Their Teachers?

Given the urgency of children's psychosocial needs during the middle grades years and their vulnerability to the debilitating effects of rejection and abuse, no one questions the importance of their feeling cared about and respected by the adults in their lives. Young adolescents scrutinize more carefully than ever the dispositions and idiosyncrasies of the grownups they're responsible to. So, to a great extent, it is warranted to assert that no matter what textbooks, materials, curriculum guides, and such are employed, the teachers are the curriculum. Therefore, working out comfortable, secure, interpersonal relationships between adolescents and adults is a high priority.

Sadly, however, many teachers of young adolescents dislike their work (Carnegie Council on Adolescent Development 1989). The variable, transitional character of youngsters' needs, priorities, and behaviors during these years is often unsettling to adults whose interests and disposition fit more comfortably with younger children or more mature adolescents. Many teachers serving in the middle grades have not been appropriately prepared for working with these students, and they do not understand what is involved in creating responsive educational programs. Rigid expectations and assumptions better suited to teachers of older students have for too long misled many of those who wound up assigned to the middle grades.

On the brighter side, though, are the many teachers who, in spite of not having been prepared for middle level assignments, have found a great deal of satisfaction and intrigue in their work. One study of teachers who "like to teach in the middle grades" showed that the developmental characteristics of students at this level was a primary attraction and source of satisfaction (Carr 1989). When teachers are dispositionally suited for this work, they make valuable contributions to youngsters' lives, from which they accrue the satisfying benefits of professional efficacy.

To those who are suited for teaching early adolescents, we need to provide specialized preservice teacher education programs. In fact, the number of such specialized undergraduate programs has been gradually increasing (Alexander and McEwin 1989a). The Carnegie Task Force strongly recommends programs that focus on interdisciplinary, developmental approaches to the education of young adolescents, including at least two academic concentrations. They further recommend that candidates interact with and observe middle level students beginning in the candidates' freshman year and continuing through graduation, after which they would continue on in a paid apprenticeship that would lead to a license once all requirements are met (Carnegie Council on Adolescent Development 1989).

Teachers who are already in the field and who wish to stay there need continuing professional education. In fact, never before in the history of modern American education has there been a greater need than now for teacher re-education. Even the post-Sputnik national urgency for reforming the preparation of science and mathematics teachers pales in the light of the need for expert middle level educators who are prepared for and committed to helping youngsters who are experiencing the life-threatening exigencies of contemporary adolescence.

The rapid growth of professional associations at state and national levels during the last two decades speaks to the urgency teachers themselves feel for further education. If teachers are to support the reconceptualization of schooling at this level, they must more fully understand the nature of both early adolescence and exemplary, responsive schooling for this age group. And not just in response to changing certification requirements; they must also show initiative and take responsibility for their own professional growth.

What Do Students Want from Their Teachers?

We can only offer broad generalizations about what young adolescents want from their teachers. A single list of requirements would be impossible to construct, given the increasing differences among children during this period of immense change and the substantial differences of school culture in, say, the inner city and rural settings. But in light of needs associated with the changes that youngsters experience, it is possible to make some generalizations (Ames, Ilg, and Baker 1988). Also, informal inquiries to find out what students like and dislike about teachers and which teaching practices help and hinder their learning can further clarify valued teacher attributes (Stevenson 1986). How youngsters perceive their teachers is a worthwhile topic for classroom and school inquiry.

For the most part, during the years from approximately 10 through 12 or 13, youngsters tend to be more concerned about teachers' personal attributes than teaching skills or how much teachers know. This compares with younger students who are preoccupied with how congenial and agreeable their teachers are. Beane and Lipka's (1986) study of adolescents who had done well in school grouped students' positive descriptors of preferred teachers under one word: "nice." While this term may be difficult to define to the satisfaction of researchers, students and adults both intuitively understand.

Some data suggest that as youngsters progress from the 5th through 9th grades, the percentage of students who believe "my teachers care a lot about me" declines (Benson, Williams, and Johnson 1987). Whereas approximately half of the 5th graders claim that it's "often true that their teachers care about them," four years later only three out of ten express the same belief. Less formal classroom inquiries carried out by middle grades teachers suggest that personal characteristics and attitude toward students has enormous influence on how students perceive their teachers. Only 8th graders give very much attention to teachers' technical abilities as instructors (Stevenson 1986).

What, then, given the enormous variability from student to student and one community to another, can we confidently claim about young adolescents' needs and wants of their teachers? The following teacher traits are desired by students of all ages, but they are especially critical to children in the middle grades.

Respect

Middle level students want and need to believe in their teachers. Teachers, on the other hand, must earn that respect. They must conduct themselves appropriately. A teacher's real authority, at least in the eyes of middle grades students, exudes two-way respect. Respected teachers don't just verbalize what they believe, they demonstrate their values in their interactions with students, fellow teachers, and people in the community. In the vernacular of the streets, kids take notice when "teachers don't just talk that talk—they walk that walk."

In their bifocal study of a Japanese junior high school, Paul George (1989) and his son Evan compared their observations of some differences between Japanese and American middle level education. A 7th grader at the time, Evan made a noteworthy observation of a fundamental cultural difference: "The Japanese students respected adults a lot more than American kids do. Like on field trips, the boys that I expected to cut up were really calm, took it seriously. They even held the doors and were really polite to the adults—to any adults, not just the teachers."

The study goes on to report that discipline problems are virtually unknown, and Japanese young adolescent students relate to each other and adults in ways most American teachers would love. They are more commonly submissive to adults. Habitual courtesies and conformity to a single set of norms was probably much more typical of young adolescents in earlier years of American education, too. But contemporary life, for whatever reasons, no longer provides such homogeneity. Respect for adults has to be earned, sometimes over and over. Young adolescents pay careful attention to how they are treated by adults and in whom they invest their esteem.

Teachers who earn and enjoy the respect of their students are the ones who show their understanding and prove themselves and their maturity as they skillfully use patient but direct intervention and prudent retreat. They give their students clear messages that they are understood and that their issues are taken seriously. These teachers are worthy models for their students' deference. And their students recognize and respond accordingly.

Fairness

Development of reasoning from "childhood moralism to the ideological convictions of adolescence" heightens young adolescents' consciousness of justice and fair play (Erikson 1968). Nothing is more likely to alienate students than a perception that a teacher has been unfair or caters to favorites or dispenses recognition and approval capriciously. Students' sharpening attentiveness to how things are supposed to work, to what the rules are, and to how much "wiggle room" exists can cause distinct challenges for teachers.

As people who are continually conscious of equity in their relationships at school and who daily make judgments involving classmates, youngsters also crave opportunities to help establish the rules or procedures they will live by. Teachers who listen to the perceptions, interpretations, and concerns of their students, and who are willing to negotiate without abdicating appropriate authority, communicate humanity and rationality. For too long we have accepted the notion that teachers must handle discipline alone. So-called "good teachers" were those who controlled students through threat or intimidation. Now, however, learning about and using mediation techniques for students to resolve interpersonal conflicts has become an effective, appropriate strategy for involving young adolescents in dealing constructively with their interpersonal differences. Teacher-student relationships built on qualities of equity, fair play, and turnabout are reciprocated in the ways in which students respond to teachers who are fair to them.

Safety

Kids are very perceptive about how schools and classrooms are supposed to work. They recognize when a teacher is struggling for order. And it's not uncommon for them to exploit such a situation by seeing how far they or a classmate can push the teacher before real consequences come down. Part of the challenge is to test the teacher; part of it springs from the need to test oneself, one's nerve. There seems to be a contradiction in the fact that, on the one hand, youngsters want structure and a teacher who keeps order while, on the other hand, they won't hesitate to exploit a teacher's weakness. Ultimate respect depends on how the teacher answers this test. Students may still like a teacher who can't maintain control, but it's much more difficult for them to conduct themselves respectfully. They seek the safety of knowing where lines are drawn and what consequences will result from violations. They value order, consistency, and fair play.

Trustworthiness

Changes in social pressures and resulting stresses in early adolescence bring out new anxieties about who can be trusted. This apprehension is well-documented by David Elkind as a form of "peer shock . . . betrayal" (1984). As interpersonal relationships take on new and unfamiliar conditions, fear of betrayal intensifies.

Youngsters learn from experience to be careful with whom they trust their private thoughts. They are particularly anxious about whether or not confidences shared with peers are secure. Squabbles between two or more kids over the divulgence of a private communication are common. Teachers, too, must prove their trustworthiness. They must be mature, sensitive, and discreet even in their informal dialogue with students. Youngsters need not only someone they respect but someone who they believe is sympathetic, worthy of confidence, and who can be relied on as an advocate.

Sense of Humor

Arguably, the most heavily used positive descriptor of anything young adolescents experience, particularly in reference to school, is "fun." That word covers an array of experiences, but it is especially employed to describe favorite teachers. In scores of interviews we've carried out with young adolescents, "fun" refers most often to a mix of "good humor" and "sense of humor." When teachers use their own wit in ways that don't belittle or bewilder, they may effectively break up tension that otherwise can become disrupting. Puns seem to be particularly popular, perhaps because many students are developing the intellectual skill necessary to create and exchange them with teachers.

Another dimension of teachers' good-humor/sense-of-humor identity derives from what they find funny that their students also enjoy. Comedies in movie theaters and on television may amuse both generations. Mutually enjoyed comic strips such as *Garfield* and *The Far Side* also create a bond of humor that students value in the teachers they prefer. Safe, nonexploitive humor shared between adults and students can become a conduit that bonds their spirits.

Achievable Challenges

The middle level education movement of the last several decades has made pedagogy far more responsive to the developmental needs of young adolescents. An important frame of reference for understanding youngsters' shifting intellectual development has been the work of Swiss psychologist Jean Piaget, who focused on children's thought processes. A central concept of Piaget's theory is "equilibration," a process by which we draw from our previous experience in making and remaking the mental structures that constitute our understanding (Inhelder and Piaget 1958). Healthy intellectual growth during early adolescence is in large measure a blending of what is already known or understood with manageable new experiences. Helping to facilitate that blending in the classroom is a complex but critical challenge for teachers.

Uppermost in kids' identity needs at this time is the desire to be competent, to be doers and producers, and to be known by others by what they do well (Erikson 1968). Educators who recognize the normality of students' craving for success and recognition create curriculum designs and instructional strategies that are directed toward accomplishing equilibration and ensuring successes for all students. Students appreciate and value teachers who help them become successful in ways that establish their individual worth and respectability in the eyes of peers and their parents. Teachers who teach by helping students in these ways represent the very best of their profession.

Teachers also serve children particularly well when their standards and learning challenges require students to stretch themselves to succeed, so long as the degree of stretching is within students' reach. Tasks that frustrate or overwhelm serve no constructive purpose. When learning tasks are confounding, many students withdraw, sometimes quitting altogether and becoming alienated from school learning. Much of the dropping out of older adolescents appears to be rooted in academic frustrations and alienation in the middle grades (Wheelock and Dorman 1988). Assignments and responsibilities that confront youngsters with tasks and objectives within the reach of their potential at the time are the ones that stimulate commitment and effort. As youngsters learn to manage these challenges successfully, their self-confidence grows and they develop healthy mental attitudes. Students appreciate teachers who set such expectations and follow up with whatever support is necessary.

This account of students' needs and preferences in teachers is not exhaustive, of course. Every thinking person knows that in addition to these basic needs are many unique, personal situations that produce singular needs. Young adolescents in our schools reflect the exceptional variety of family backgrounds and community influences that is reflected in our pluralistic society. They represent exceptionally diverse economic backgrounds, family contexts, circumstances of personal health and hygiene, and psychological conditions. Responsive teachers attempt to recognize and meet idiosyncratic needs as much as possible, aware that the relationship they have with their students may be critical to each child's life, now and later.

What Do Teachers Need and Want?

Many teachers of young adolescents today dislike their work. Assignment to a middle grades school is, all too frequently, the last choice of teachers who are prepared for elementary and secondary education. Teachers view duty in the middle grades as a way station (Carnegie 1989, p. 58).

John Goodlad's now-classic study, *A Place Called School* (1984), also showed career disenchantment at the middle level. Junior high school teachers experienced less career fulfillment than their elementary and high school counterparts. Joan Lipsitz, summarizing her study of four successful middle schools, offered, "One essential ingredient that is not always replicable but should be: (teachers) must want to be where they are" (1984, p. 200). Traditional schooling practices that have not served young adolescent students well have also failed to satisfy many of their teachers.

Yet many middle level teachers are flourishing in their work (Lipsitz 1984, Carr 1989). We know hundreds of teachers who thrive in working at this level. They are committed, highly competent professionals who love their work.

How is it that so many teachers can be disappointed while others have found their professional niche and want to stay right where they are? The question begs for further research. Despite limited formal data, we are nonetheless able to identify some characteristics common among those middle level teachers whom we see doing spectacular work and enjoying it. They seem to have found compatibility between their own needs and wants and the developmental needs and interests of young adolescents.

Generalizing about teachers' wants and needs is no less problematical than doing the same thing for adolescents. Just as youngsters' priorities and capacities change as they develop, teachers' understandings of their work and personal predilections also evolve as they mature in their careers (Glickman 1985). Beginning teachers, for example, tend to have quite different agendas from those of mid-career teachers and teachers approaching retirement. Yet there is something transcendent about teacher and student priorities at the middle level that invites informed speculation based on research and our many years of personal experience working with teachers.

Early in the current middle level movement, William Alexander pointed out that "it is the nature of the student . . . which differentiates teaching in the middle school from any other level" (Alexander et al. 1968, p. 83). One study of middle school and junior high school teachers reported that teachers with the greatest understanding of adolescent development preferred teaching at the middle level, while teachers with the least understanding would prefer to teach at another level (Timmer 1977). Obviously, adults who do not understand young adolescent interests and natural behaviors or who understand but find them personally objectionable should not become their teachers.

One study based on principals' reports indicated that the most important reason for their teachers' having chosen to work at the middle level was their desire to work with pre-adolescents and young adolescents (Brown and Howard 1972). In another study of "very best teams" that also solicited principals' views, teachers on their best teams were described as embodying "respect, understanding, commitment . . . in their relationships with their students." The principals in this study (George and Stevenson 1989) commonly said of their teachers: "They work at understanding their kids." "They accept all kids, and they don't give up on them." "They treat their kids like customers." Even though the research examining motivation and vocational satisfaction of middle level teachers is limited, it is safe to say that middle level teachers who are satisfied in their work enjoy working with students in developmental transition.

Next arises the question, "What are the specific elements of young adolescent development that appear to attract teachers to this work and retain their interest and commitment?" From our day-to-day work in schools, we have come to recognize some themes.

Energy and Enthusiasm

People who have been around young adolescents know that these young-sters possess lots of intellectual energy and vitality as well as physical vigor. "They keep me young!" say teachers. Their energy is directed to school projects, their social milieu, the arts, and sports. Above all, they want to do things, and the doing is active. As one teacher said, "It's as if I've entered a revolving door before them, but they get out ahead of me."

Some teachers consciously chose this age group, knowing the potential for sustaining their own personal energy levels. It appears that authentic, personal energy exchanges and enthusiasm for life and learning are key motivators for teachers who consciously choose to work with this age group. Reciprocal energy exchanges that can occur in middle level schools draw them to this work and sustain them in it.

Curiosity

Teachers know that young adolescents are by nature curious about an abundance of diverse things. Thus they are generally motivated for learning. Successful middle level teachers seem to welcome the inevitable challenges that accompany the naturally broad spectrum of students' interests, shifting passions, variable attention spans, and wide differences in intellectual sophistication. Middle school teacher Ross Burkhardt once commented, and several colleagues agreed, "Ultimately, I don't think it really matters very much what we teach so long as the kids are learning and feeling successful at school." The emphasis was primarily on students developing as satisfied learners. This view of the academic curriculum was not as nihilistic as it may sound. At the moment this comment was made, the teachers who were engaged in the conversation were surrounded by students responsibly busy at an array of studies and projects. Those of us who have worked with young adolescents on a sustained basis understand the pleasure of being a party to curiosity that breeds initiative and responsibility.

Not all middle level teachers see their task accordingly, however. Another teacher in another school, bitter toward his 7th graders because half of them were getting an F in his science class, grumbled, "My job is to separate the sheep from the goats, not to mollycoddle kids." This individual represents the constituency referred to by Goodlad and in the Carnegie report, a constituency that is frustrated, even antagonized, by youngsters who don't conform to expectations more appropriate for older students.

Collaboration and Cooperation

Doing things well while working with others not only helps create situational understanding and cooperation, it also helps cultivate an atmosphere of unity and mutual pride. The epitome of excellence in a sport such as professional basketball is that successful teams don't just win games. They also demonstrate teamwork and selfless play. Excellence in the performance of a string quartet reflects the musicians' common interpretation of the score and commitment to a harmonious unity. Teams such as these transcend perfunctory individual performances, no matter how outstanding any solo effort might be.

Middle schools at their best set aside the tradition of exaggerated competition commonly associated with secondary schools. Consequently, they offer important new opportunities for collaboration. Teachers on effective middle level teams value the bonding that evolves among the adult team members (George and Stevenson 1989). And they prize collaborations with students on tasks that have been cooperatively defined and carried out (Carr 1989). Such intangibles grow naturally from activities that involve both generations in exploratory, firsthand learning. Common goals, close communication, and mutual support can be cultivated more easily in settings where interdependence is a primary goal, whether the players are athletes, musicians, or teachers.

Another relationship possibility that appeals to many middle level teachers is the potential for establishing close communication and collaborations with students' parents and other community members. Reengaging families and community members in the education of young adolescents has become an urgent, immediate priority (Carnegie 1989). Excellent teams are known for their initiative in developing such alliances (George and Stevenson 1989). Empathetic teachers have a timely opportunity to forge new roles and alliances with the public.

Varying Curriculum and Instruction

Although students go through essentially the same developmental transitions, individual dissimilarities at any moment are normal and to be expected. Although two youngsters may be best friends and spend all of their free time together, they may differ substantially in physical size and intellectual sophistication. Their developmental variability needs to be complemented by variety in instructional approaches and the curriculum content teachers select.

Middle level teachers who were prepared for secondary teaching bring expertise from at least one content area. Yet in responding to interdisciplinary opportunities appropriate for young adolescent students, curriculum is not always confined to single-discipline approaches. Attention should also be given to building interdisciplinary understandings (Vars 1987).

For example, consider Allen, a middle level teacher with a secondary science background who was participating in his team's planning for an interdisciplinary unit on "Community." Because of his knowledge of bees, Allen could draw on content and concepts not only from his natural science background but also from his knowledge of graphic arts, geometry, health, economics, and sociology. Working collaboratively to design integrated curriculum units is intellectually stimulating and provides opportunities for learning from colleagues. It also frees teachers from the illusion that every student must cover the same things at the same time in the same way.

Excellence in teaching at the middle level emphasizes teaching and learning by doing. Regardless of whether the content comes from a traditional, single-discipline approach or is an interdisciplinary creation, pedagogy emphasizes firsthand contact, individual interpretation, and diverse ways of representing knowledge. More routinized teacher behaviors such as lectures, textbooks, and worksheets still have a limited place, but they are tempered and balanced with topical studies and learning activities that are adaptable and responsive to individual learning styles.

Overlapping Work and Play

For too many years, too many middle level educators have been misled by an exaggerated, false dichotomy of work versus play. Expert teachers know that when young adolescents are involved in authentic learning, such distinctions blur. Work is acknowledged as a good thing. True learning includes elements of work with the delights of play. True satisfaction with one's own learning includes the knowledge that success is a result of commitment, effort, and sometimes sacrifice.

Expert teachers do not value excellence any less than their colleagues elsewhere, but they may define it differently. Equating excellence to a particular cutoff point between a grade of A or B or "passing and failing" is a hideaway for simplistic thinking. While expert middle level teachers appreciate and promote academic integrity, they assess achievement in light of students' developmental capabilities. These teachers know that laughter and even whimsy have a place in their students' experience.

To Make a Difference

The ultimate affirmation for any teacher is the assurance that students are better off because of who you are and what you do. This is not fantasy or self-delusion for middle level teachers who are responsive to student needs. They know whether or not they are contributing meaningfully by how their students develop. At this level of schooling, where multi-age grouping through teaming is possible, teachers also learn that working with the same students for more than a single year enhances the opportunity to witness student growth (George, Spreul, and Moorefield 1986). There are more opportunities to get to know each other well through advisories and teaming in a middle level school that is organized to build this kind of connectedness. Teachers also learn that relationships they build with students embody potential for trust that can become an enduring resource for both generations.

These incentives for middle level teachers do not constitute a complete list, only some of the central, interpersonal possibilities they seek when choosing to teach at this level. The crux of that choice, however, lies in the nature of the relationship teachers aspire to have with their students. Teachers who know themselves to be a comfortable match to the personality traits and dispositions of young adolescents bring a special empathy to their work. Their enduring commitment is to their students.

Traits Evident in Healthy Student-Teacher Relationships

A recurring misfortune in middle level education is that teachers and students so often miss opportunities to form positive, lasting relationships. The tyranny of daily schedules and the need to cover six to eight periods of subject matter in a day make it almost impossible for adults and students to have adequate time together to build relationships on familiarity, understanding, and trust. Circumstances are improving in many, many schools, however, through responsive organizational arrangements such as interdisciplinary teaming and advisories. Yet opportunity alone is not enough. Most teachers also need support in understanding how their roles and responsibilities should be redefined.

With the movement to reconceptualize and reorganize middle level education well under way, it must be recognized that teachers working in changing schools need a great deal of help and support as they go about rethinking what they do. It is not uncommon for experienced teachers to react warily or adversely to arguments and proposals that appeal for change. Teachers who prepared to teach a particular discipline are often aggravated, even angered, by new expectations that were not part of the original commitment they made to teaching.

But change also benefits teachers who want their interpersonal relationships to go beyond the roles defined by subject matter obligations. Teachers, like anyone else weighing change, want to know, "What does this mean for me?" Thus, it is appropriate to conclude this chapter by identifying several themes that characterize the best of teacher-student relationships.

The Essence of Understanding Lies in Listening and Talking

Teachers must not assume that kids understand and accept them and their agenda. This is more than a truism. It is an appeal to educators to exercise the disposition and take the time to earnestly engage students in regular, open conversation. If there is a single great deficiency in middle level education, it is that we teachers become so preoccupied with our curricular agenda that we lose sight of our supposed beneficiaries, of who they are and what they believe and care about. The best communication is characterized by careful listening, thoughtful reflection, and taking turns. It is equally appropriate, perhaps even necessary, for adults to candidly convey their questions and puzzlements. In doing so, they share their humanity. The sure products of such a climate are relationships that matter and endure over time.

Optimism and Positivism Breed Success

This statement is not just a happy thought. It reminds us that underneath the shyness or bravado of all emerging adolescents, there are vulnerable human beings, hungry for the adults in their world to believe in them and their worth. No claim is made here that if a teacher simply communicates confidence and encouragement, a child can overcome any academic difficulty. Yet many youngsters rise to the occasion when they

are buttressed by others' confidence. The emphasis here is on the promise that, with the teacher's earnest support and good cheer, the relationship that teacher and student share will be successful. In the final analysis, it is the relationship that affects young adolescents' enduring values
and humanity.

Enjoying Students Is Good

Often middle level teachers are ambivalent about having a good time
with their students. They relish the friendships, but they feel uncertain
about relaxing the more detached posture associated with a teacher's
traditional role. Respect and honor between adults and children derive
from associations encompassing genuine mutual interests and fun, times
that are meaningful for both generations. Enjoying students does not take
the place of relationships that are strictly adult, just as adult friendships
do not replace students' values and needs for peer relationships. Exclu-
sivity remains, but a valuable overlap is also achieved when teachers
find genuine enjoyment from time invested with their students.

Authority Is Rational

Affection, nurturance, democratic control, and inductive discipline promote healthy development in young adolescents. Authoritarian control,
coercive discipline, the withdrawal of love, and permissive control in-
hibit healthy development (Benson et al. 1987). An unwritten law has
presumed that teachers have to maintain distance from students in order
to preserve their authority. On the other hand, young adolescents are
coming to understand democratic authority. It is predictable that they
should expect that the only good authority is rational authority. Authority that is good must be rational if it is to receive genuine respect. And
respect is earned through unpretentious dialogue, earnest exchanges of
ideas and values, and a joint commitment to democratic processes, especially when differences of perception deny consensus.

Young adolescents who naturally question or challenge the way things
are need grownups who understand their development and who appreciate the richness of thought they invest in their propositions and alternatives. These young people also often need forgiveness and a fresh start,
but there should never be any doubt or question about who is and must
ultimately be in charge. Yet adults must demonstrate their enlightenment
about authority and their maturity by listening earnestly, encouraging

and weighing students' perceptions, and patiently explaining their own rationality.

∎   ∎   ∎

Teachers who freely choose to work at the middle level, as well as those who may find themselves stuck there by circumstances they cannot control, need to look on their student constituency as partners and accomplices in an effort to make living and learning as rewarding as possible. They must not just acknowledge the legitimate claims students make for respect, safety, and reasonableness; they must energize their commitment with investments of time, patience, and good humor that evidence their trustworthiness. We will all do well to remember that in our relationships with youngsters, as in our relationships with each other, what goes around comes around. If we want a better society for future generations, we have to build it now through the trusting relationships we build with youngsters and the humanity we represent.

We must do it now.

3

Middle School Organization: Values Underlying Practices

We have seen schools that, while having adopted many of the organizational arrangements of exemplary middle level schools, remain unyielding to students' developmental needs because adults have not made the requisite personal investment. These schools are middle schools in name only. We have also seen traditionally organized junior high schools where teachers are personally attentive and responsive, in spite of organizational and instructional limitations. Alive in many of these schools is a deliberate shifting toward more responsive organizational formats and practices. The middle school movement of the last three decades has encouraged more and more schools to bring together social and instructional organization and a responsive human spirit. As the following vignettes illustrate, the future is promising.

■　■　■

The Paradise Project, a two-teacher, fifty-student team at Edmunds Middle School, is well known throughout the school and community for the quality of its publications. In addition to the core curriculum, these 7th and 8th graders also study journalism. They work with many different literary forms, but their trademark is journalistic reporting. They produce the school newspaper, the Edmunds Examiner, and Noun, a biannual literary magazine. Larry and Eric, the teachers, have worked together for twelve years. Their journalism curriculum has evolved to include peer supervision strategies that enable the 8th graders to conduct much of the direct instruction. In one-teach-one fashion, older students pass along their insights and share their composition and critiquing skills under the expert eyes of their teachers.

Over the years, Larry and Eric have managed to acquire some essential publishing equipment, such as electric typewriters, Macintosh computers, word processing and page layout software, duplicating equipment, and other office supplies. Their two classrooms and two smaller wing rooms are organized to include a publications office with a telephone, an elaborate filing system, production tables, and storage.

Publication deadlines are as much a part of the team's weekly routine as anything else. Thursday visitors are impressed with the students' deliberateness and efficiency as they work to complete the weekly edition of the Edmunds Examiner, which is distributed through advisory groups every Friday morning.

■   ■   ■

In a K–8 school in an urban area of Massachusetts, students on a 6th-, 7th-, and 8th-grade multi-age team carry out "orbital studies" as part of a curricular requirement for membership on the team. The goal of orbital studies is for each student to work at becoming an expert on a topic of the student's choice. Teachers, who serve as consultants for the team, rarely veto a student's topic; they are more concerned about students becoming comfortable with the academic process of choosing a topic, designing a plan for learning, becoming an expert among peers, and subsequently demonstrating their knowledge to interested classmates, teachers, and parents.

Orbital studies last from three to six weeks, depending on the topic and the student. Topics have included a history of stamps, tuning a two-cycle snowmobile engine, Robert E. Lee's battles in the Civil War, building a kayak, constructing a family tree for Tolkien's Lord of the Rings trilogy, aircraft of World War II, black holes, danger to dolphins, quilting, cuisine of Venezuela (the student was a recent immigrant), Boston bridges, extrasensory perception, and Maine conchology. The primary goal is for each student to experience the feeling of personal dignity from achieving expertise—regardless of the subject matter.

■ ■ ■

At the Folsom School in rural Vermont, a team of seventy 11-, 12-, and 13-year-olds carry out assorted tasks related to an interdisciplinary study of "The Story of Flight." Over a week's time, each student compiled a personal documentary record of the team's study and participated in a group project. For example, in their groups, the students:

- interviewed a retired apple farmer about the benefits and costs of spraying and dusting by airplane.
- interviewed the mother of a 1st grader about her career as a flight attendant.
- tested paper airplane designs for distance, flying time, and accuracy. They recorded the results of each test flight on clipboard data sheets and later entered the information into a computer spreadsheet program that a teacher helped them create.
- studied and compared cloud formations depicted in the meteorological section of a primer on navigation as they created representations for a bulletin board.
- annotated significant advances in the evolution of human flight on a timeline stretched across a wall in their classroom.

The four core teachers on the team plus the special education teacher, the librarian, and the physical education teacher joined together to plan and coordinate some three dozen activities from which their students could choose in approaching their individual studies of the topic.

At the beginning of the unit, team members volunteered for specific tasks. Several weeks later they began to meet daily to assess, evaluate, and make necessary adjustments. A surprise was added as part of the unit's conclusion: A parachutist from a local skydiving club landed on the soccer field during recess so that students could interview him about his hobby.

■ ■ ■

Bonnie teaches physical education to 7th and 8th graders in a union secondary school in New England. Her husband, Joe, is a 7th grade English teacher in the same school.

Near the end of the second week of the new school year, Bonnie invited nine of her students—members of her advisory group—to a Friday evening outing with her family at their health club. The children were excited and curious; this would be the first time any of them had ever been inside a health club. After some initial self-consciousness, they delighted in using the exercise equipment and the pool.

Two hours of casual physical activities and conversation generated a comfortable familiarity among the adults and children. Bonnie and Joe made great strides in developing the quality of trust and respect that 12-year-olds need from the adults closest to them. These students learned about the human side of their teachers: their backgrounds, the things they like to do in their leisure time, and what they value in their lives outside the school as well as within it. And they learned about Bonnie and Joe's family—their two children, the interests they share, their rituals and traditions, something of their own childhoods, how they had met, and so on. Bonnie also learned about the youngsters she was responsible for as advisees in this happy, neutral setting.

On their way home later, Bonnie and Joe recounted the evening's simple enjoyments and the perceptions they had gained of each child as a distinct person with unique ideas, interests, and hopes. Although there were no formal goals or agenda for the evening other than to become better acquainted, everyone left with new understandings of each other and a positive experience that would provide the foundation for lots of future interactions.

■   ■   ■

The Lawton School, organized for grades 6-8, was scheduled to begin receiving 5th graders because of crowded classes in the feeder elementary schools. During the year prior to this change, teachers on the 6th grade team discussed ways they might help facilitate the entry of the younger students.

One teacher, Peter, conducted an inquiry in his classes to find out what his students had been concerned about a few months earlier when they were new students entering Lawton. Using the results of his inquiry, Peter and Beverly, a teammate, designed a language arts unit in which students would create a "Handbook for New Students." Kids talked a lot about what it had been like when they were new students at Lawton. Then they wrote essays about their fears and offered advice about how to adjust to a new school with older, bigger kids, new teachers, and unfamiliar routines.

A few weeks before the end of the school year, when the handbook was complete and ready for distribution, small groups of 6th graders took turns visiting their old elementary schools to distribute the hand- books to 4th and 5th graders who would be attending Lawton for the first time next fall. They showed Lawton in a positive light and eagerly solicited and answered questions. Since Peter's inquiry had pointed out that one of the three major worries of incoming students had to do with working combination locks, it was decided to offer the incoming kids a lock and combination to take home on the last day of school so they could practice over the summer.

■ ■ ■

Every Friday and just before holidays, the 118 7th graders and five teachers who make up the Adventurer Team at Lawton School begin the day with a 40-minute All-Team Meeting, attended by the team's five advisory groups and led by a student moderator. The moderator's job rotates weekly among the advisory groups.

Teachers participate in All-Team Meetings with the same rights and responsibilities as their students. Sometimes the moderator calls on a teacher for an interpretation or advice, but the teachers generally save observations and suggestions until they can offer feedback in private. They work with their students more closely in the advisory groups and help them learn how to preside over the larger meeting with their peers.

The purpose of the All-Team meeting is to take care of team busi- ness; the students report on plans for special events, solicit volunteers for projects and committees, and clarify questions or issues. Meetings also give the kids the chance to enjoy each other's imagination and humor; singing and skits—often parodying their own lives—are common fare. And they're occasions for teachers to recognize students' achievements in school, sports, and outside activities such as scouting and Little League. Especially valued by the students is the "BIG A" certificate, which recognizes students' initiative and contributions to the Adventurer Team.

At the All-Team Meeting on the Friday prior to Columbus Day, four committees (Parade and Costumes, Booth, Refreshment, and Clean-up) report their suggestions for the upcoming Halloween Fair the team is giving for children at the Mt. Zion Church Day Care Center two blocks away. This is the third year the Adventurers have helped at the center by reading stories and leading games. But this is the first time the team has undertaken as large a responsibility as the Halloween Fair. The agenda moves smoothly, however, and there is time for singing. The meeting ends after four students dressed as spooks move through the crowd handing out cards designating needs and tasks that students can volunteer to work on at the fair.

■ ■ ■

Values and Practices: A Sampler

Compelling organizational models for middle schools have been offered in recent years (Lipsitz 1984), although no single paradigm is mandated for this level of schooling. Rather, an exemplary middle level education is best understood as a fine cloth composed of deliberately selected threads—actualized values and distinctive practices that occur and recur—forming a strong, durable fabric. Not just any fabric will do. We must not confuse burlap with linen or muslin with silk. The fabric that supports exemplary middle level education is a tight, carefully conceived and executed blend of some essential threads.

The preceding vignettes may be likened to the designs and patterns the colonial seamstress stitched in creating a sampler— a display of her imagination, artistry, and skill. No matter what designs her stitchery composed, she carefully worked them through and onto the warp and weft of the fabric. Just as no two samplers are exactly alike, neither are any two schools or programs within schools exactly alike. Just as the seamstress created an original work of art, exemplary individual schools are organized to reflect the originality of the educators working in their distinct context. With the anecdotal stitches of this chapter in mind, let's examine the composition of the fabric for those threads of recurrent values and underlying practices.

Primary Threads—The Warp

Exemplary middle schools and textiles are similar in that they are both constructed around and on some primary threads that establish the patterns by which coherence and continuity can be seen and demonstrated. In weaving, primary threads are the warp. In organizations such as schools, primary threads are values articulated in the organization's philosophy and mission. Ideal middle schools embrace one overarching value from which all other value statements and practices derive: They are organized in ways that correspond as much as possible to the distinct developmental needs of youngsters between the ages of 10 and 15.

This agreeable resolution has generated some innovative ideas about how to organize middle schools—ideas that now have evolved into practices that are more responsive to a wider array of student needs than has been characteristic of traditional junior high schools. Middle level educators all concur about the necessity of schooling that is student-needs-responsive.

But creating needs-responsive schools is a highly complex matter. Traditional concerns about covering the curriculum and teaching the basics usually get in the way. The issue is exacerbated by the magnitude of young adolescents' diversity and their ever-changing needs. Thus it is particularly impressive that exemplary middle level education includes so many excellent examples of schooling that are student-needs-responsive.

The developmental exigencies of the young adolescent years have been comprehensively identified and discussed (Erikson 1986, C. James 1974, Elkind 1984). The rest of this chapter describes the instructional and social organizational values and practices commonly found in exemplary, needs-responsive middle schools.

In light of the wants and needs of both young adolescents and their teachers, organizers of exemplary middle schools have created or adapted designs to increase the possibility, if not the probability, that adults and young adolescents will come together to work for their mutual support. These plans, in terms of vision and spirit, are more akin to an elementary school orientation than to traditional high schools. Yet they are also established components of a distinctly middle school organization (Alexander and George 1981, Eichorn 1966).

Cross Threads—The Weft

"Only primary threads do not a fabric make." Similarly, schools are not "made" merely by organizational schemes. The organizational arrangements become viable only through people's actions. The values and commitments of those who work within exemplary middle schools constitute the cross threads—the weft. It is the binding of warp and weft that gives substance, texture, and strength to the whole. Cross threads are spun from resilient strands of basic human spirit and character, attitudes and expectations about the potential of formal education, and considerable physical and spiritual effort. Although the fabric of a school may be initially woven by adults, the cross threads that bring the fabric to ultimate completion in the best of middle school education are those subsequently manifested by students when they likewise represent the same human values in their day-to-day school lives.

Values Underlying Practices in Exemplary, Needs-Responsive Schools

Students' Healthy Growth and Development are Paramount

The fundamental rationale for schooling at the middle level is to foster healthy personal and academic growth and development of students during their young adolescent years. Teachers who embrace the vision that sound development is uppermost also understand and accommodate child development. In reviewing recurrent themes of successful schools in her classic study, Joan Lipsitz (1984) observed that attaining each characteristic of successful schools depends on recognizing and working with pressing aspects of growth and development during early adolescence.

Teachers are able, therefore, to assess individual student growth from an enlightened frame of reference. Student progress through various developmental tasks is carefully monitored so that teachers are continuously informed about what their students can and cannot do, as well as what they know and what they do not know that they need to know.

Drawing from these insights, teachers make considered adaptations for their students rather than shifting the entire burden for adaptation to them. Knowledgeable teachers are also well-acquainted with their students' special interests, activities, talents, and social dispositions. The ongoing value, then, reflects the goal that all students will achieve individual potential, both now and later as responsible adult members of society.

Optimism and Positiveness Prevail

The uninitiated visitor to an exemplary middle school is typically amazed by the civility of interpersonal relationships. People get along amiably; they know that what is going on is working. Jim Garvin (1987) writes about truly effective middle level teachers in terms of their belief in themselves, in their students, and in what they teach. The work teachers do bears out these values, which in turn affect what students are willing to believe about themselves and their potentials.

Good will among students and between adults and youngsters is the norm, as is an atmosphere of general confidence about the propriety and worth of academics. Students recognize that their teachers are convinced about the value of what they teach. In such a responsive setting, they are more inclined to buy into academic commitments. Such a positive work ethic is a product of the youngsters' successes and belief in themselves as learners. This ethic suffuses the school's intellectual life as well as ongoing, day-to-day, interpersonal affairs.

High Expectations Abound

Again, teachers expect more from their students because their experience tells them that what they are doing works (Lipsitz 1984). Success breeds higher expectations, which lead to greater success. The expectations are as tied to teachers' assessment of their own performance as to their students' performance.

Just as teachers have high expectations for success and are optimistic about the schooling they are part of, they seek high standards for themselves and their students. Students are expected to be curious and to become competent, savvy learners who engage problems and ideas rather than ignore or avoid them. Student commitment to self-improvement, to developing a work ethic that is resolute and self-disciplined, and to responsible participation in the school community is a high priority. Teachers are well-read. They openly share their intellectual, aesthetic, and athletic interests.

Adults Understand and Support the School's Mission

The most outspoken interpreters and advocates of any organization are those who understand, believe in, and support its mission. In recent years, this commitment to mission has been shown to be central to successful corporations (Peters and Waterman 1982). An equivalent loyalty to the mission of schooling based on the developmental needs of young adolescents is also a trademark in exemplary middle level education. In successful schools Lipsitz (1984) observed a willingness and ability to adapt all school practices to individual differences in the intellectual, biological, and social maturation of the students.

Passion and good humor signal personal commitments to programs and people. Although there may be differing degrees of enthusiasm for individual components of the mission, disagreements do not become divisive and destructive in the best of middle schools. Teachers take ownership of the school's purposes and programs as true professionals must, and they help parents understand and support them.

Teachers Believe They Make a Difference

Teachers are confident that they can make a difference in youngsters' lives. They are relentless in achieving a union of success because they have affirmed that they are the right person to do it! They don't give up on students. They believe in their potential; and even though they may not see the fruits of their labor, they know that they have planted the seeds (Garvin 1987).

Belief in the propriety and efficacy of one's work is a powerful motivator. Students and teachers in truly excellent schools know they are part of something very special, and they convey that strong value in the vital work they do. Teachers recognize that their commission is much more inclusive than the traditional stereotype of perpetually dispensing subject matter and conducting recitations. They value the realization that they are enabling youngsters to grow in confidence and competence as learners and full citizens not just in their generation but in the larger world. Academic self-sufficiency, personal stability, tenacity, patience, loyalty—qualities that reflect healthy maturity—are welcome evidence to teachers who enjoy the certainty that their service and persona are making important differences for their students.

People Are Empowered

A long-held, familiar criticism of American schooling is that, while students must learn about democracy in school, they aren't allowed any meaningful participation until they enter the adult world. Teachers have likewise historically complained that they are powerless to change schooling because they must answer to a host of external authorities: administrators, schedules, parents, and the state.

Shared decision making is necessary in order for teachers to commit themselves to the total school program and mission. Social and instructional organizational schemes involve decisions that are natural priorities for teachers and best decided collaboratively. Exemplary middle schools employ collaborative decision making not only to achieve the best results, but to assure professionals that they are empowered to make decisions affecting their professional work. Meaningful collaborative decision making also carries over into students' school lives. Where youngsters learn to exercise authority, they also learn real responsibility. Experiences that enable all participants to resolve questions affecting their school lives foster respect and appreciation for the values of the democratic process.

People Pull Together

Although competition has long been argued as essential to motivation, the truth is that successful cooperation actually produces more benefits and is, in the final analysis, more compelling. We often overlook the fact that we live in the most cooperative society ever realized; and cooperation skills have become highly prized in industry and community life. At its best, cooperation produces both individual and group benefits that are greater than those derived only from competitive relationships.

Excellent middle schools where collaboration has become the dominant goal reflect this realization through collateral decision making. Successful teams function collaboratively to make decisions and act on them. Students and teachers choose cooperative mediation processes to resolve interpersonal conflicts.

Principals Lead by Example

Principals of exemplary middle schools are remarkable people who have earned their authority and influence by successfully leading colleagues in the manifestation of each of these seven qualities. They model the same egalitarian, cooperative approaches to building a climate for collaboration that they expect teachers to use in the educational program. Highly successful principals see their major function to be instructional leadership and securing autonomy for the schools in their districts (Lipsitz 1984). They lead by constantly exemplifying commitment to their colleagues, their common vision, and shared decision making. They lead with patience as they hurry toward clear, mutually understood destinations. In the spirit of the expression, "what goes around comes around," teachers, like these principals, also work at modeling through their teaching, values, and behaviors the same qualities they aspire to for their students.

Conditions Promote Innovations

Teachers in the opening vignettes were either blessed with supportive opportunities from the outset or they worked collaboratively to achieve enough latitude and authority that they were empowered to reconceptualize their circumstances. But how did they get their visions? What steps did they follow to establish their programs? How did they deal with organizational inertia? These questions center around values and practices that constitute a framework for planning and implementing a social and instructional organization characteristic of exemplary middle schools.

For example, when two or more teachers prepare to work as teams, they need assurance that they will be responsible for a single group of students. The Paradise Team, the Unit Team, and the Adventurers in the opening vignettes were organized so that teachers could work solely with the students on their teams. Teaming fails when those in charge fail to realize the fundamental differences between teaming and departmental organization (Erb and Doda 1989). Cross-team participation by core teachers is almost certain to be divisive because one teacher inevitably needs more focused responsibilities.

Another typical condition is the lack of enough time for students and teachers to accomplish everything they are expected to do plus all the things they want to do. Time is a precious, finite commodity that, when scheduled or regulated externally, may only create an illusion of order at a costly price of misapplication. In order to get the greatest benefit from this limited resource, it is necessary for teachers to apportion available instructional time for their teams.

This does not mean, of course, that teams decide what time the school day begins and ends or when their team will have lunch or go to physical education. Of necessity, they recognize the importance of a master schedule to accommodate teachers, programs, and activities that are schoolwide.

What teams are able to do is organize large blocks of time according to their instructional priorities. For example, a two- or three-hour block of time that is not interrupted by the master schedule can be organized any number of ways. If the teachers have planned an interdisciplinary unit, they can schedule more time for activities they know will take longer. The Unit Team manages to reserve the morning hours every day for what they refer to as "prime time." When they're involved in a major interdisciplinary unit, the students are able to spend all of their morning hours on it whenever necessary, while other students go about their work according to different priorities.

There are constant, organic tensions between externally defined curricular requirements and student or teacher interests. There is a lot more worth learning and teaching than can be accommodated under the constraints of school days and resources. It is essential for continuity and coherence, therefore, that teachers organize the curricular program as they see fit. They apply their knowledge about their students' readiness for particular developmental tasks and their knowledge of curriculum possibilities to create curricular studies that are needs-responsive. Student readiness and interest in particular topics are structured according to teachers' knowledge of needed skills, as well as possible content structures and activities.

Teams need to engage the democratic process as a participatory enterprise. It would be illegal and unethical for them to ignore or reject laws and policies established by their communities and school boards. However, within the broad scope of established systemwide policies and procedures, teachers and students work democratically to establish their own system of governance.

Change That Works and Lasts Is Owned by the Changers

Educators who aspire to student-responsive programs, and who take responsibility for advancing their own professional growth, continuously examine their work and look for examples of the best of contemporary practice. They read about, visit, and study successful teams or projects in other schools while reflecting on the strengths and deficiencies of their existing programs. They assess students not just in terms of grades and scores but for their enthusiasm for learning and citizenship and by creating innovative projects in their own classrooms. These are the values and behaviors that reflect a professional attitude of commitment to go beyond even the best of current practice.

The Adventurers' All-Team Meeting is one example of a process for collaborative decision making in which students participate. By creating a forum for discussing and deciding some of the issues that affected students, self-governance became a living value. It is important to stress again that such arrangements do not mean that the educators forgive their authority and responsibility to carry out the laws and policies of the community and the school system. The issue being addressed here is that of self-governance vis-a-vis community decisions such as team policies, procedures, and rules. Not only are students able to conceptualize a process, they learn how to responsibly participate in it.

Exemplary Schools: Artful Innovation

Like the colonial seamstress who fashioned samplers that are still appreciated today, educators who practice artful innovation offer a vital embodiment of their values through their craft. Those who would prescribe any single recipe for organizing any single school would do well to rationally examine the exceptionally rich variety of practices reflecting the values of middle level educators. These include interdisciplinary teams, advisory programs, a balanced curriculum, team scheduling, and other practices discussed in the next chapter, as the warp of the fabric of exemplary middle level education. These practices form an exceptional array of original creations.

4

■

Middle School Organization: Practices Reflecting Values

When team leaders from the Smyth County, Virginia, middle schools met to begin a curriculum study, there was some general doubt about what could be accomplished. It was not the first time some of the team leaders had taken a look at the curriculum. Many had served on accreditation teams in years past, and a few had been on state task forces that examined subjects, objectives, and courses. Some had just taken a college class on middle school curriculum and instruction and had some new ideas about how curriculum could be arranged.

One of the teachers who had been involved in a similar project agreed to take the lead, although a consultant was on hand to help serve as a resource. The consultant took an unusual approach to curriculum evaluation. She asked, "What questions would we need to have answered if we were to do a thorough study of your middle level curriculum?" (At least she hadn't begun with the idea that there had to be a definition of curriculum before anything else could take place!)

The team leaders were timid at first, but finally someone suggested that they begin with a look at the subject areas to be taught. So the first question revolved around what to do about language arts, social studies, math, and science—a question the group soon realized was too broad and too narrow at the same time. It was too broad in that these subjects comprised most of the course of study in the middle

---

46

grades. It was too narrow because it didn't look beyond the immediate or what was already being done. Why did they always have to start with the subject areas, anyway? Why couldn't they look at the bigger picture? The consultant asked if this curriculum was supposed to reflect the expectations of the high school and tidy up anything that hadn't been taught at the elementary school, or was there some freedom?

The leader of the exploratory team then stated that they should go about their curriculum study differently this time. She asked, "What is the most appropriate role for home arts, woodshop, music, art, and those types of subjects in the middle school curriculum?"

When confusion seemed to obscure their efforts, the consultant reminded them that the task, at least initially, was just to raise questions, not to feel they had to be in any order, or even that they had to be answered. So the team leaders decided to randomly generate some questions that each had been considering before the meeting. They had thought of curriculum in terms of subjects for so long that their first questions naturally reflected a subject-centered focus: In language arts, to what extent should students leaving the middle school be able to understand and respond to written or spoken language? How well should they be able to express their feelings, thoughts, ideas, and experiences so that others can understand them? What is this idea of cultural literacy, and is it the real objective for language arts?

For math, they asked to what extent students should demonstrate mastery of fractions, decimals, ratios, proportions, and the like. Should algebra, which requires more abstraction, be included? Is the idea of mathematical competence appropriate?

The social studies people wanted to ask how much students should know about people, work, culture, environment, and geography. How could students best learn about cultural pluralism within their own state, locale, and region? Does social studies imply a sensitivity to other cultures? Should social studies really be an investigation of global citizenship?

A science teacher raised several issues: Should the science curriculum deal with discrete and traditional investigations into earth, physical, and life sciences? Shouldn't science emphasize science-related careers, local scientific resources, and the current status of technology? If "cultural literacy" is the goal for language arts, is it possible that the middle school science curriculum might be summed up in the context of "scientific literacy"?

The team leaders got caught up in the action and began to move beyond the subject areas. They suggested other questions: Exactly what are the basic skills students need to master? Should credits earned at the middle school count at the high school? Should there be any multi-aged classes in the curriculum? What should be done about the students who fail one or more of the curriculum areas? Should they be retained? Should the exploratory curriculum really reflect breadth, and should everyone be able to take any of the subjects offered in the school? What about the band students who can take only one exploratory because they're locked in to the band period? Should the program (they had now dropped "curriculum" in favor of "program") have hands-on experiences throughout or just in the customary exploratory subjects?

They generated more than thirty questions and then decided that most of them were not really answerable.

They sat back and took stock. Their problem, it seemed, was that they really didn't have a definition for curriculum. Was it a course of study? Was it all the subjects taught in school? Was it more than merely the subjects? What was this thing called curriculum?

After several more hours of spirited discussion, the group arrived at a definition of curriculum that all could support to some degree: Curriculum is the sum of all the experiences children have because they attend school. This definition surprised them in several ways: It was much broader than any they might have considered at the beginning of the discussion. Also, they were taken aback at how many of their questions weren't answerable, at least not in isolation. They would need input from the senior high as well as the elementary schools. And the questions would have to be considered in relation to each other. They had created a kind of Chinese menu that let them have one choice from column A and two from column B, but that eliminated any from column C. Who would have thought there were so many questions to be asked in the first place? And who would have thought that so few could be decided solely by these middle school team leaders?

They became even more intensely involved when they tried to decide exactly what areas of the curriculum they really had any control over. Considering the state mandates, the board of education's expectations, and history and precedence, could they really change anything? Or were they locked into doing business as usual?

The discussions eventually wound to a meaningful conclusion. The team leaders agreed that middle schools have considerable control over how teachers teach and how the program is delivered. Teachers and administrators have a fairly wide degree of freedom in structuring and carrying out their programs. Team leaders, staff, and administrators can decide on the best way to deliver the desired content to students. They left the meeting with at least one clear thought about curriculum: They would take control of what they could control. They would focus their study on how to provide the best delivery model possible as well as how to cover the expected content. They would ensure that, as far as possible, all the experiences children have because they attended their middle school would be the best these adults could give.

■ ■ ■

There are seven practices reflecting the basic middle school values discussed earlier. These practices are:

- Setting the context and climate for learning
- Establishing guidance and advisory groups
- Promoting team identity and belonging
- Teaching through interdisciplinary exploration
- Effectively organizing time and space
- Advocating multicultural awareness
- Integrating the school and community

Setting the Context and Climate for Learning

Harry Stanfield, principal of East Cary Middle School in Raleigh, North Carolina, began the school year with an impassioned speech to his faculty. Harry spoke of his vision for the school and his commitment to young adolescents. He talked about dealing with human growth and development, his concept of failure and how it could be avoided, and his hope for relationships between students and teachers. Most eloquently, though, Harry said about the school:

> I hope for a school that is a safe place for students and employees to work. I see East Cary Middle School as a place that helps young adolescents move safely onto the plains of adulthood with the skills and the self-confidence to choose the best roads in life. I know that we will all be proud when we say, "In this corner of the world, the children are secure and I helped make it so" (Stanfield 1990, p. 45).

Jim Garvin is executive director of the New England League of Middle Schools and former president of the National Middle School Association.

In a conversation about his research with parents, he described some misconceptions of educators about the reasons parents send their children to school. According to Garvin, we have the mistaken idea that parents are concerned about grades and academics, the content of the curriculum. His research found something very different and quite interesting.

Garvin surveyed over a thousand parents and asked them, "What would you like the middle level school to provide for your child?" In order of preference: Parents first want to know that their children are safe. Then they want their children to know at least one adult well enough to go to when they need support. Third, they want to know that the school is concerned about helping children develop constructive friendships. They want the curriculum to include opportunities for children to get involved in activities; and they want their children to have had enough good experiences to want to return the next day. Then, *after* all of that, parents want a curriculum that will give children what they need to know to be prepared for high school.

Garvin drew some personal conclusions from the data. He was struck by the importance parents attached to a healthy school climate:

> If students go to school and feel safe, if when they get there they know well a teacher or two, have some constructive friendships, are involved in activities, and have some positive, intellectual experiences, won't students want to return to this school the next day? Not only will that student want to return the next day, but these experiences have a high probability of creating the kind of climate that will bring about increased achievement. These days, when we are looking for support for middle school programs, we need to inform parents about early adolescence and then show them how our programs accommodate those needs (Garvin 1987, p. 4).

Garvin discovered what parents want when they send their children to school. Teachers want much the same things for their students. They are concerned about safety and security. They want eager learners who are excited about studying the curriculum at hand. Everyone wants a positive ethos and a climate conducive to greater success.

Over the doors to the offices of the Middle School of the Kennebunks in Maine are large, block letters that read: **WE CARE ABOUT KIDS**. The truth of that motto is evident throughout the building: photographs documenting projects, displays of students' work, jovial interaction among people of all ages about countless topics. Visitors are bombarded with undeniable evidence that this school is a wonderful place for people to be.

Many of America's schools have finally overcome a tradition, apparently rooted in the Puritan ethic, that school should be a place of austerity and travail. Having fun does not necessarily violate an atmosphere of serious, purposeful work that is so clearly present in the best middle schools. To the extent that programs include activities calculated to comply with students' need for fun, American education has made some progress in humanizing institutional education. We have a rapidly growing number of schools that are genuinely responsive to the developmental conditions of the students they purport to serve. Even a casual visitor to schools like Kennebunk quickly senses the character of relationships between adults and children in a school where both generations work deliberately to create a supportive and productive school climate. In truly needs-responsive schools, the ambience tells students and adults alike: "This is a good place, a safe place, a place created for you."

Whether or not these values are articulated in the school's philosophy, they are the true beliefs at work in such a place. And they are easily recognizable. Visitors judge schools by observing how people deal with each other; they look for evidence of teachers' attentiveness to students and their work, the care reflected in the decor and condition of the facility, and the balance of ease and seriousness with which people carry out their work.

Orderliness is an especially trustworthy indicator of school climate. It is characterized by a feeling of relaxation and ease of movement. Although rules may be posted, something more profound than impersonal directives is at work. It is the outcome of people recognizing the inherent benefits of civility and voluntary order.

Humanitarian and academic standards are taught by calling students' attention to each other's efforts. Displays of all types of student work and interest proliferate. Whether it's an essay, a clay pot, a geometric design, or a baseball card collection, work is displayed to recognize and celebrate students and their accomplishments and interests. Student recognition is further given through awards for outstanding performance, model citizenship, or academic improvement. Student-of-the-Week or Teacher-of-the-Week bulletin boards recognize people by identifying their interests and personalities. The prevailing theme is to "celebrate people."

Beyond these immediate evidences of a positive atmosphere, school climate is further enhanced by students' and teachers' activities. Curricular programs such as peer tutoring, peer counseling, and conflict resolution through student mediation demonstrate the ways in which students take responsibility for themselves and each other. As an outcome of their efforts to restructure for the coming century, the Kennebunk faculty experimented with an intergenerational summer camp that brought together toddlers, senior citizens, and the generations between them. The camp gave young adolescents an opportunity to teach and learn from people of all ages and backgrounds somewhat different from their own. When groups of students commit themselves to working for their mutual benefit, the forecast becomes "sunny and warm."

Additional schoolwide activities reflect intentions to match the school program to the nature of young adolescents: academic competitions such as spelling or geography bees; problem-solving contests such as designing model airplanes or hot air balloons; and dress-up days such as Backward Day or Masquerade Day. Talent shows, lip-sync contests, carnivals and fairs, and theme events such as Biography Week or Technology Day also vary the opportunities that enrich students' and teachers' lives as they plan and carry out activities together.

Another important indicator of school climate is the way the school accommodates students' rapidly emerging interest in the opposite sex. Prudent schools provide well-organized, chaperoned parties that include games, videos, and other activities, as well as an introduction to dancing, so that youngsters can find comfortable ways to participate and learn about themselves and one another in social contexts, without undue pressure.

In schools that have a nurturing, positive climate, students and teachers deliberately commit themselves to each other. Adults initiate most activities to complement students' needs and wants. Students respond to the adult lead with initiative and cooperation. There is no single prescription for such a climate, just as there is no prescription for love or peace. It is the product of patient nurturing and persistence.

Schools committed to a context and climate for learning recognize the value of a smooth transition from the elementary school, with its secure and self-contained environment, to the usually larger and more impersonal middle school. They know this can be a scary experience for students. Talking with middle graders, especially 6th graders, we find many who don't look forward to having to go "up" there. Who will help them? Who will know if things aren't going well? Who can they talk to? Who will be their teacher? What if they can't open their lockers?

Some schools provide a ready answer for these questions and try to allay kids' fears. Lorna Glant (1989) is principal of Madison Elementary School in Marshall, Michigan. Madison is a transitional school for all 4th and 5th graders in the district, who then go on to Madison Middle School for grades 6-8. Glant hears many students talk about their fears regarding middle school. They tell her they're afraid someone will beat them up or that they'll miss lunch. Others worry about getting lost because the school is so big; others fear missing the bus. In some cases the combination lock is the greatest fear. For others it's not knowing the teacher or where to go the first day.

So Glant and her colleagues at the middle school have set up a rather extensive orientation curriculum to give incoming students a more accurate perspective of what the school is really like. They want to reduce student anxiety, increase communication between the two staffs, and educate parents about the middle school program and site. The faculty of the two schools work together to coordinate a student visitation day at Madison Middle School. Teachers hold a pre-visitation "team" meeting and a pre-visitation orientation. The principal of Madison Middle School sends a letter home with the students listing the accomplishments of children in the higher grades and the things the younger students can look forward to.

Visitation day arrives and the excitement far overrides the fears. There are color-coded name tags, upper-grade buddies, and lots of tour guides. Once at the middle school, students meet some of the administrators and counselors for some insight into how things work and what exciting activities are planned in the new school. According to Glant, the "Move to the Middle" program has replaced fear with anticipation, and a great deal of misery is avoided.

Arcola Intermediate School in Morristown, Pennsylvania, also has a comprehensive orientation program for incoming 6th graders. According to Andrew Case (1989), Arcola's principal, the program begins with an effort to pair visiting 5th graders with host 6th graders. On visitation day, 5th graders become 6th graders and share the real 6th grader's daily experience. They go to the locker with their partners, attend classes, take quizzes, and go to lunch. Back in their own school, the 5th grade teachers provide time for students to discuss their experiences and perceptions of the new school.

Another very important part of the program is a visit the intermediate school counselors make to the 5th grades each May. Much important information is shared between the 5th grade teachers and the counselors, who serve as spokespersons for the 6th grade team teachers. In June, the intermediate administrators go to each of the 5th grade classes and meet with the incoming students over breakfast, in the students' own territory. In August, the intermediate school faculty puts on a full-day orientation for all interested parties. Parents can meet with their child's teachers, learn about the activities of the school, and find out more about the interdisciplinary teams.

Principal Case is very sure that the orientation program is well worth the effort. He is so convinced that the activity is a success that he does much the same thing in cooperation with the secondary faculty and administration to smooth the 8th graders' transition to high school. While not as complex, their orientation does have a buddy program with a 9th grader and an instructional class visit. The transitions are smoother and the anxieties reduced for everyone.

> So we begin to answer some of the students' questions and concerns about the new school through an orientation. But what about their fears that they won't know their teacher or that no one will know them? We answer by saying that, based on what we know about middle graders' development and what we know about the nature of schools for students this age, we're going to help find a "friend in residence," a teacher advisor, a home-based teacher, and an ombudsman for each student. An effective middle school demonstrates "middle-schoolness" by providing an advisory program for all its students.

Establishing Guidance and Advisory Groups

During their first few years of school, youngsters become accustomed to self-contained classrooms. They think of themselves as belonging to a single class and teacher, and when they need adult help, they go to their teacher. Kids also get to know each other, and "our class" becomes a reference for friendship. Teachers, too, develop feelings of belonging toward their students and acquire broader understanding of their children when they spend an entire year together.

Reconfiguring teachers and students according to departmental organization usually occurs between the 5th and 8th grades. Planning shifts more heavily to subject matter priorities, especially the college-prep courses. This organizational change also shifts teachers' orientation from more holistic notions of children's needs to an emphasis on covering content. Teacher guidance tips more heavily toward academics, thus reducing the previous attention to balancing academic growth with everything else. This one organizational change does more than anything else to put at risk the interpersonal familiarity that children and teachers have come to count on.

Exemplary middle schools have found a way not just to preserve valued guidance relationships but to formalize and enrich them. The essential step in helping people to quickly get to know each other well is to ensure regular contact through small advisory groups, generally referred to as "TA" for "Teacher Advisory" or "AA" for "Advisor-Advisee" (M. James 1986). Although these groups meet daily for just fifteen or twenty minutes, they provide students with a touchstone group of peers and one adult to which they belong, and they give teachers access to students and time to begin building partnerships. They also create a climate and a context for teacher-student relationships that establish a standard of helping that in the best of circumstances carries through the rest of the school program.

These groups do not usurp the more specialized services rendered by guidance counselors. Teacher-advisors cannot replace formal guidance but should, in fact, augment it. In circumstances that call for the expertise of a trained guidance specialist, teachers who are knowledgeable about their advisees can make referrals on matters that might otherwise be overlooked.

The paramount benefit of advisories is that they constitute the student's first line of belonging—a group one belongs *with* rather than *to* (C. James 1974)—thus meeting the child's need for a strong affiliation with a group of peers within the school. It can become a forum for conversations about events in the school and in the world, about getting along successfully at school, about fashions and sports teams and fads and music. Much of what is talked about in advisories emerges from the children's interests and questions. Ethical questions are welcome for study, contemplation, and resolution. The essence of an ideal advisory is responsible judgment and decision making by students who feel they can safely and candidly discuss issues important to their welfare.

In addition to the scheduled advisory group meeting during the school day, groups often make plans to socialize and study together or take on school or community projects such as decorating a bulletin board, planting trees on Arbor Day, participating in a fund-raising walkathon, and so forth. These projects enhance students self-respect and build citizenship values.

The advisory group is also an appropriate place to address tobacco, alcohol, and drug use. Although these issues are usually included in the health curriculum, discussing them in the advisory adds to the school's comprehensive response to what has become a catastrophic risk to the health and welfare of young adolescents. The greater intimacy of communication in well-established small groups increases the chances for every student to have a say. And because middle level teachers are expected to be current in these topics, specialists aren't required. Teachers who are the most knowledgeable, most often guidance personnel or health educators, commonly serve as tutors or coaches for their colleagues.

Drug, alcohol, and tobacco education in the curriculum also provides an opportunity for attending to how students make decisions. There is no better school setting than the advisory group for examining personal decision making. Well-established group dynamics should ensure a constructive climate in which students can gain an accurate, comprehensive understanding about how these stimulants work and become addictive. Clarifying ethical dimensions as well as creating an atmosphere of mutual support for responsible action are further enhanced by the healthy group dynamics that middle level kids and teachers seek.

Another notable benefit of advisories is that teachers become well informed about each of the students in their group and can share their knowledge with colleagues to support students' well-being. Teachers often mediate problems between their advisees and other teachers and function as the school's primary liaison with parents. Teachers are the conduit for distributing academic reports and memorandums. School-wide parent meetings and routine parent conferences are often organized by advisory groups.

The ultimate rationale for the host of activities advisories may carry out is utterly simple. The gist of it lies in building intergenerational partnerships based on mutual understanding, advocacy, and loyalty—elements that are critical to youngsters' intrinsic needs to feel safe, connected to other kids, and sure that at least one teacher is acting conscientiously as a personal mentor. Where these traits exist, healthy growth, development, and personal satisfactions flourish for students and teachers alike.

Early adolescence is characterized by a great need for personal development and the enhancement of self-esteem. Students need to seek information about themselves in a positive, nonthreatening, and non-graded environment. Middle graders need to associate with adults in mature but still somewhat protected ways. While this happens to some extent in regular classes, there is always the barrier of the grade and the teacher's expectations in light of the subject matter. In the advisory it is more relaxed and more personal.

Students also need an opportunity to work with and learn how to get along with other students. Much of their personal development is done by comparing themselves with others in their age group. According to Lipka (1989), young adolescents have a powerful drive to form relationships with peers and find a niche in the group. They need experiences based on cooperation, not competition, and for cooperative reward structures. In classes, this comparison is often done only academically. In advisory, there is much more attention to personal growth and to different types of individual success. According to NASSP's James Keefe, "Personalization is the key to making schools exciting and productive places of learning," (1986, p. 85). Keefe contends that the advisement program is the heart of personalization.

Research that supports the advisory curriculum comes from varied sources. Connors and Irvin (1989) found that 51 percent of schools identified as excellent have an advisor/advisee program. This contrasts to only 31 percent of their randomly selected middle level schools. To the degree that middle-schoolness indicates excellence, an advisory program becomes a central program component.

In a survey of 672 schools nationwide to determine what types of schools and programs best match young adolescents' needs, Cawelti (1988) found that middle schools are far more likely to provide program characteristics needed by young adolescents and to use teacher-advisor programs. In other research, Alexander and McEwin (1989) concluded that there was more use of home-based guidance (advisory) in middle schools than in other organizations. Putbrese (1989) surveyed 3,400 students who indicated that advisory programs improve teacher-student relationships on a personal level. They give students a greater sense of control and promote an atmosphere of equality. Being part of an advisory improves students' ability to share their feelings and appears to reduce smoking and alcohol use and abuse. Putbrese's study also found that advisory programs help students develop their more altruistic natures.

Another benefit of the teacher-based advisory curriculum is directed toward at-risk students. Jerry Dawson (1987), assistant principal at Fleming Middle School in Grants Pass, Oregon, believes at-risk students should be reached at the middle level, before they enter high school. His school has developed a formal identification process, a schoolwide discipline program, and a three-year homeroom class.

This class, Fleming's version of the teacher advisory, is called FACS—Family, Advising, Community, and School. In addition to helping teachers get to know students in an informal setting, the Fleming program sponsors volunteer adult mentors who assist at-risk students, a dynamic youth services team, an early work experience, and a "gram" program for staff members to send home good-news notes about students. Fleming also has a comprehensive retention intervention program and firmly established goals for the school, including "removing labels from all students, promoting student self-concept, and mastery of the academic basics by all students" (Dawson 1987, p. 85). According to Dawson, "the challenges of helping today's at-risk youth seem overwhelming, but they can be met head on. We are helped in meeting those challenges whenever we see our school slogan, 'I am a teacher—I deal in futures'" (p. 88).

Another example of the advisory program in action is Sarasota (Florida) County's PRIME TIME, consisting of a 30-minute advisor-advisee period at the beginning of each school day. Two or three days each week are allocated to guidance activities and group interests, while other days are for silent reading, journal writing, exploratory activities, and community projects.

To help teachers become more skilled with guidance-based groups, Sarasota County offers a training program consisting of ten 30- to 45-minute modules (Myrick, Highland, and Highland 1986). The PRIME TIME teachers who have participated in the training sessions say they gained a greater ability to tune into and respond to student feelings and to use effective questioning techniques and a combination of high facilitative responses. They're more confident about leading PRIME TIME groups, and they're more aware of the factors that lead to effective teaching and helping relationships.

At W. S. Parker Middle School in Reading, Massachusetts, John Delaney (1986) and his faculty worked many hours to devise an advisory to help guide students through difficult times and difficult decisions. They decided on a home-based guidance program as a logical and important part of the overall curriculum. The program consists of several processes. First, the advisor and students take care of all the details of new-student orientation. Then the school engages in a major effort to make students feel a sense of belonging. Once this has been accomplished, other goals are targeted, such as improving study habits and preparing for tests; building self-esteem; accepting responsibility; and understanding expectations, decisions and their consequences, and relationships.

For Delaney, making the point that home-based guidance teachers are a great deal more than attendance takers is critical. Students stay with the same guidance teacher all three years, and the teacher is encouraged to play the role of surrogate parent. To help teachers accomplish this, Delaney has a support system and monitoring process. Meetings are held to share successful approaches and answer questions; resource packets are available; and time is spent during team, departmental, and faculty meetings to discuss specific students from various teachers' perspectives.

Promoting Team Identity and Belonging

During these years, many youngsters show a particular need to belong to an identifiable peer group known, for example, for its unconventional clothing, hair styles, language, or behavior patterns. They sometimes subordinate their personal or family identity to the icons of their chosen group. In light of the powerful need to belong to a peer group and the enormous social change youngsters encounter, such behavior is understandable.

Most of us gain some security from knowing and being accepted by other people in our group. Children, too, regardless of what may be happening in their families or schools, derive feelings of safety and reassurance from knowing they're part of an accepting, approving peer group (C. James 1974). Satisfying their needs to belong also helps offset children's anxieties about anonymity, which are inevitable in schools with large student populations who may be defined solely in terms of a grade level, a homeroom, or the entire school.

One way to broaden opportunities for group membership is to organize students and teachers in teams. The Carnegie Council on Adolescent Development (1989) has recommended that middle schools "create small communities for learning where stable, close, mutually respectful relationships with adults and peers are fundamental. . . ." Studies of successful teams have revealed a number of common organizational features, beliefs, and practices (George and Stevenson 1989, Erb and Doda 1989).

Teams can be any size, but they are usually made up of 50 to 120 students and two to five teachers whose major responsibilities are to the team. Members of the team, both students and teachers, spend most of their school time together. Students may be assigned to teams randomly or on the basis of some selected criteria. Grouping by particular intellectual attributes is not appropriate, however, since it could lead to discrimination and rivalry destructive to school climate. Teams should reflect a natural mix of students: girls and boys, gifted and learning disabled, all in the same grade or multigrade.

Teams are interdisciplinary in that the teachers are usually responsible for one or two disciplines and are qualified to handle the basic curriculum. Sometimes the team may be augmented by special education teachers or teachers in the arts or physical education who also teach off-team students.

Teaming optimizes the potential for all the team members to become acquainted with each other. The team constitutes an extended family of sorts within which students can form primary social affiliations. Team identities are usually enhanced by a team name, logo, motto, colors, mascot, rules, awards, rituals, traditions, and so on. Team meetings become forums for learning democratic processes. Awards, celebrations, plays, contests, and a host of one-of-a-kind projects further convey the team as a community that is worthwhile, stands for good things, and supports its members. At its best, the team serves as a positive answer for students' need to belong to a sanctioned and defined social group.

Teachers on teams benefit from knowing students and their parents more fully and sharing insights and ideas with other teachers who are equally involved. Being responsible for fewer students for more of the school day enables teachers to recognize and more fully address students' indigenous conditions and needs. The team format helps teachers maintain more continuity and coherence in the academic program and allows for more flexible coordination than can be achieved within the traditional departmental organization.

Eight essential issues are common to interdisciplinary teams as they plan their social and instructional organization. These issues, presented here as questions, are also appropriate to use as criteria for ongoing program assessment and possible redirection.

Who are we and what do we stand for? For a clear definition of any team, its members need to clearly spell out the beliefs, goals, and standards the team represents. A written mission statement complete with goals, pledges/mottoes, and a handbook of team procedures clarifies these issues. A logo representing team values, a team mascot, colors, a variety of apparel such as tee shirts and caps, and other school paraphernalia including pins, patches, book covers, and the like help students identify with the team. Daily rituals, regular team meetings, special events, and traditional activities commemorating important days further flesh out team identity and presence as a definable entity.

How do we decide? Spelling out procedures to be followed in making decisions is essential. Most decisions the teachers will make, especially about details, are likely to be consensual. It is still necessary, however, to have a clear procedure for resolving differences. Determining team leadership is especially important, for that individual will be responsible for the single most critical function in successful teaming: open, candid communication. Difficult issues will arise from time to time, and team unity will be essential to the best resolution.

It is likewise necessary to develop an all-team decision-making process so students will understand the rules for their participation and become skillful at group processes. The All-Team meeting described earlier is an example of a format that was created by teachers and employed as a weekly forum for students to address an agenda they help create. This way of deciding helps students learn from direct instruction as well as observing each other's performance. They learn to lead as well as follow. As they learn how to fairly and democratically resolve differences in viewpoints on team issues, they become more savvy about participatory democracy.

How are we organized? A master schedule that preserves teaming as the first priority is essential (Erb and Doda 1989). Once the master schedule is determined and team resources and membership are defined, the team itself must make some organization decisions, such as defining the roles of team leader, administrative liaison, and parent liaison and selecting individuals to serve in them. Frequently, the largest single task team members confront is establishing a day-to-day and week-to-week schedule that will enable them to accomplish multiple goals. Ample advance time for team preparation is essential, especially for new teams. Administrative support and encouragement are critical because teams are almost certain to encounter challenging difficulties that force disappointing compromises. Strategies must be worked out for maintaining the kind of communication with the administration that ensures understanding and fosters support.

One especially essential component of the team schedule is arranging a common planning time each day so that teachers will be able to deal with the host of details concerning, for example, academic standards, all-team meetings, interdisciplinary studies, grouping decisions, evaluation and grading methods, record keeping, and policy on homework. Unpredictable contingencies that require time for collective study and resolution will also arise. Team governance may appear overwhelming at first, but as teams gain experience and grow, more and more of the initial details become absorbed and the team develops to more advanced phases (George 1982).

How will we keep everyone informed? Effective communication among all the constituents of a team is vital; and that link begins with the need for clarity among and between teachers and students. Additional essential links are those between the team and the administration, between team teachers and off-team colleagues, between teachers and parents. Talk is the primary mode, and teachers on highly effective teams meet regularly with administrators and parents. Excellent teams keep parents informed through regular meetings and special events for parents on the team, parent conferences, and teacher-initiated telephone conversations. Written and documentary records are also necessary. Files of student work and anecdotal accounts of progress are often maintained so that the focus of discussions about student progress includes tangible work.

Written records of team meetings and periodic team newsletters are constructive ways to make sure that everyone associated with the team has a way to keep up with the team's functioning.

What and how shall we learn? Once organizational procedures have been worked out, defining the academic program is the most critical step in the team process. Defining the nucleus of that program, however, is more than simply rehashing existing curriculum guides or meekly accepting district or state guidelines as the final word. In a real sense, the team must *invent* their curriculum by identifying what has been mandated and then augmenting that framework with further studies they wish to emphasize.

The inclusion of orbital studies and the study of flight are examples of innovations created by a particular group of teachers who recognized possibilities for extending students' interests and cultivating accessible resources in ways that enriched students' learning. Such emphases reflect the often idiosyncratic interests and specialties of team members, and these excellent teams are also identified outside their team by these distinctive academic pursuits.

How will we know what's being accomplished? Given the variety and extent of the activity of an effective team, systems for keeping up with student progress are essential. Mere grades in a grade book are inadequate and atypical of the best teams. Emphasis is on richer, qualitative records, such as individual documentation, anecdotal records, and student record keeping. Regular communication between teachers and advisees provides a steady flow of data about how a program is working.

Evaluation of the team itself is an ongoing formative process. Teachers assess the effectiveness of what they are doing by exchanging observations on a day-to-day basis. Formal team evaluation may be conducted periodically, just as school assessments are, using many of the same criteria. Shadow studies or other formal observation structures can provide useful team evaluation feedback. Visits with colleagues, middle level specialists, or even parents are another way to assess the team's progress.

How will we celebrate our successes? A framework for recognizing accomplishments is critical to team momentum. Regular awards ceremonies are one way to recognize students' academic accomplishment, their citizenship on the team, and their contributions to others who may or may not be on the team. Teachers can also promote team spirit by celebrating birthdays, creating features like Student-of-the Week, and observing special holidays and team traditions such as "Hat Day" and "Backward Day." Teachers need to keep in mind adolescent youngsters' need to be recognized and appreciated for their accomplishments and efforts, academic and otherwise. They also need to remember that in students' eyes, a team that is worth belonging to celebrates its members and their accomplishments in "fun" ways. The kind of fun students are referring to here usually doesn't involve trivial amusements; it is simply part of classroom experiences that are satisfying and affirming, that "feel right" to them. Teachers need to tune in to what's right for their particular students.

What's in it for us? This is not a silly question. Teachers, like students, have valid and appropriate needs that they would like to satisfy in the classroom. When teachers can honestly say that doing their best work and serving youngsters are complementary goals, they find fulfillment and new energies. In the best schools, teachers work collaboratively, challenging themselves and one another in healthy ways. They define excellence in terms of human growth and accomplishment—for adults as well as for children—and feel comfortable setting personal goals and candidly assessing their progress and satisfaction. These teachers believe that their work is professional and unique, that it matters, that children are better off for having been associated with the team and the teachers.

Teaching Through Interdisciplinary Exploration

Middle school students are naturally curious about their expanding possibilities. This stage of their lives is a time of transition, of figuring out who they are and where they belong in the world. The world outside the school, they often think, seems to be unconnected to the world of the traditional classroom, where all that matters is textbook learning and paper-and-pencil exercises. Perhaps the most important question educators must ask themselves is "How do we reconcile students' need to actively explore their connection to the world with the need for them to learn the basic academic skills that will enable them to continue their formal education?"

Effective middle schools work to provide a balance between attention to the basics, adequate coverage of necessary skills and knowledge, and the need for students to explore a wide variety of interests and experiences. Earlier models of middle grades education focused on an differentiation among students, subject-centered courses, attainment of work skills, and social and academic rehearsal for the activities of the high school. These models often included a set of teacher and community expectations for young adolescents that were not developmentally appropriate; in fact, middle school students were often treated more like small high school students. The new model of the middle school seeks to emphasize the exploration of many areas of recreational as well as academic and vocational interest.

But how do we determine what goes into this interdisciplinary curriculum? Should students have broad opportunities to explore, confined only by what the school can think of, fund, and staff? Or should they study fewer areas with more complete coverage? Other questions are pertinent here, too. For instance, should we be thinking about what is it that the children born today will need to know to live in the 21st century? Should the developmental needs of young adolescents determine the content of the curriculum? Should we be thinking about what students themselves want to learn? Howard Gardner (1989) says:

> Students want to master rules of their cultures and of its specific vocations and avocations. They want to use language precisely, not allusively: they want to draw pictures that are photographically realistic, not fanciful or abstract: and they expect a strict adherence to rules in dress, behavior, games, moral situations and other cultural activities, brooking little deviation (Gardner 1989, p. 158).

Again, in answering the questions above, the idea of a good balance comes into play. Effective schools balance depth with breadth and provide experiences that help young people become more sophisticated in the ways Gardner advocates. And they accomplish this through a mix of traditional teaching methods and methods that accommodate students' eagerness for individual choices, for firsthand experiences, and for varied learning contexts.

The Interdisciplinary Study Project. The interdisciplinary or integrated study project is one way to balance assorted concerns. In this kind of project, students study a topic as a whole, recognizing its disciplinary qualities but preserving its wholeness (Jacobs 1989). When students are encouraged to approach a topic from more than one angle, it's likely they will hit on some aspect of the topic that truly interests them, an aspect to which they can make an intellectual commitment. And when a team of teachers initiates an interdisciplinary project, students have many sources they can turn to for guidance and support, so they are less likely to fail to complete a project.

An Exploratory Curriculum. An exploratory curriculum that focuses on investigating topics firsthand through activities like interviewing, visiting, and observing also increases the likelihood that students will commit themselves to learning in more meaningful ways. For instance, Stevenson and Carr (in press) report that in one school, the study of a river that ran behind the school led one group of students and their teacher to visit a flood control dam, a sewage treatment plant, and a retirement home occupied by some of the elderly residents of a town that had been flooded by the river more than sixty years earlier. By exploring topics that students are interested in—topics that students believe relate in some way to their lives at the moment—teachers can help students make cognitive connections that are relevant and meaningful.

Independent Study. Another way to balance academic and student needs is to assign independent studies of topics that match student interests. An earlier vignette includes a list of "orbital studies" being carried out simultaneously by either individuals or small, self-selected groups of students who want to pursue common interests. Studies like these, which exemplify variety and choice, make it more likely that students will experience and pursue meaningful academic learning at this critical time in their intellectual development. Providing opportunities for independent study, of course, changes the primary role of teachers from dispensers of information to facilitators and collaborators in learning. Independent study actually helps teachers and students work together more closely to explore new interests and integrate subject matter.

Matching Young Adolescents' Developmental Needs

Middle graders are often consumed by a variety of intense, but short-lived interests. Any parent who has spent considerable money on a camera for a budding photographer will attest to this. Just about the time the camera is bought and the first role of film has been developed, the young photo-journalist has become bored with photography and now has an unquenchable desire to play the cello. This kind of behavior is normal at this age. Instead of trying to stifle it, schools can capitalize on it by offering courses or units composed of short investigations into a variety of topics. Most of us probably remember exploratory courses as classes where we actually got to do something, not just sit and listen. Of course, there wasn't much diversity—home ec or woodshop or the student council or band or choir. An interdisciplinary curriculum, however, cries out for many and varied experiences. Students can sample from a smorgasbord of experiences—they can dabble in painting, or learn how to play chess, or develop a conversational familiarity with a foreign language or two. They can play volleyball or basketball or tennis even if they aren't top-notch players.

In short, an interdisciplinary curriculum presents the middle school with an ideal means of responding to young adolescent needs. We can see just how schools are supposed to accomplish this by looking at several examples.

Smiles Across the Miles. When East meets West in the South, anything is possible. At least that's what middle school educators from New Mexico and Michigan found when they met in New Orleans and planted the seeds for Smiles Across the Miles (Wiedbusch, Tidrow-Nelson, and Johnson 1989). Smiles is a cross-cultural curriculum plan intended to help students break down their self-imposed walls of isolation and develop leadership and self-image skills.

Smiles is most simply described as a short-term exchange program that lets students travel to another school to meet their peers and learn about life in that community. The program took off when educators from Adams Middle School in Albuquerque, which is largely Hispanic, and educators from East Middle School in Ypsilanti, which has a large percentage of "at-risk" students, decided that they could build a curriculum unit out of this kind of exchange. The exchange occurred during the United Nations Week of Peace and Cultural Understanding. Teachers in both schools planned units, special topic sessions, art and music activities, and interdisciplinary activities to help the students who remained in their home school learn more about their sister school. More than 100 families were involved in this first exchange effort.

That first trip was just the beginning of Smiles. Now a monthly newsletter keeps everyone who is directly or indirectly involved with the project informed about the sister schools. And other districts are beginning to set up similar experiences based on the success of Smiles. According to the four teachers who got the program off the ground, the real value of the exchange is that it broadens the horizons of young adolescents:

> The students not only . . . learn more about themselves and the choices they make, but they learn to communicate to one another about what and how they can make a difference within their school, peer group, family, and city. The project has centered around the promotion of cultural peace and understanding while developing positive student leadership. It broadens the school curriculum and integrates the public school sector with the local community, developing a coalition that is beneficial to all involved (Wiedbusch et al. 1989, p. 41).

SEARCH. At Louisville Middle School in Colorado, what had once been a successful exploratory activities program now needed a face-lift. SEARCH, or Students' Educational Activities in Research and Creative Hobbies, had been operating for several years, giving students three thirty-minute periods every week to explore special topics. But society had changed over the years since the innovative curriculum had been implemented. The school had changed, too, doubling its enrollment and allocating resources differently. Students seemed to have different interests, and finding enough adults to teach the topics was becoming a problem. It was time for SEARCH to change too.

The faculty at Louisville sat down and brainstormed some new ideas for the program. The vision that emerged was radically different from the old program. With the help of some ninety parent volunteers, the program has been reshaped into a full-day exploratory curriculum program held once each semester. New activities range from outdoor experiences in the Colorado mountains to career investigations, such as seeing how flight attendants and pilots work at a local airline. Students can visit a high-tech computer firm, an assembly line, and a lumber mill. Some visit local colleges to see how it might feel to be a college student. Other activities include having lunch with lawmakers at the state house and touring the Denver mint. And there are always new hobbies and sports to explore.

Connie Gabel (1985), who told us about this program, says, "The key to setting up full-day exploratory activities is to know the needs of middle level students: to learn how to move beyond the constraints which can restrict the program; to have the support of the faculty, students, parents, and community; and to plan effectively" (p. 24).

Rub Elbows with Reality. According to Sam Howe (1989), a teacher writing for *Learning* magazine, experience is a powerful teacher, and hands-on activities and exploration are great assets in that teaching. In his 8th grade health class, he used rubber wounds and artificial blood to make accident scenes more real. In his 6th grade science class, students designed and built a model spaceship large enough to transport the entire class to the nearest star. In another class, they cooked hardtack, a food staple of the Revolutionary War, to test its culinary desirability.

Howe has moved into the technological age with his interest in exploration and hands-on activities still intact. Now he advocates the use of computer simulations such as *Balance of Power* and its recent update, *Balance of Power: 1990*, which places students in national leadership roles and then asks them to make policy decisions and weigh the effects of those decisions on regions of the world. In another computer simulation, students become settlers traveling along the Oregon Trail, making decisions about supplies, planning the trip, and responding to events en route. In the Field Ecology Simulation, students work just as an ecologist would in making decisions and then, after only a few minutes of work on the computer, see the impact of years of population regulations.

A Music Lab. Anthony Messina (1989) is the director of the music lab, an interactive classroom computer music workstation dedicated to electronic/computer music and related technology in the Shoreham-Wading River School District in New York. In an article in the *New England League of Middle Schools Journal,* he pokes fun at the music education establishment of thirty years ago who thought the electronic guitar was a passing fad not worthy of their attention. His hope is that the same lack of comprehension will not repeat itself with the computer-generated music of today. And his vision of the music classroom of the future surprises many people:

> It will most likely have melody, harmony, form, rhythm, words, computers and an assortment of instruments with MIDI (Musical Instrument Digital Interface) capability. Students will compose original music using this computer software in a constructivist approach to music composition (Messina 1989, p. 9).

According to Messina, middle grade students can learn music composition by doing—and he means *all* students, not just the ones who play the "right" instruments. He goes on to say:

> The computer can also help engage the reflective thinking process (metacognition) which is at the heart of any child-centered curriculum. If you take a classical approach to teaching computer music, you will surely fail. The computer should empower you to begin having "New Music" concerts in school where you can celebrate a variety of student achievements in music. Instead of one large group onstage, you may also have a number of smaller computer music ensembles. Think of the possibilities (p. 9).

A Medieval Fair. Students at Wiscasset Middle School in Maine brought the past to life in a medieval fair complete with actors, food, and pageantry (Collamore 1988). Staging the fair, complete with fifty 6th graders and their parents, was the brain child of the 6th grade teaching team, who wanted students to conceptualize this period of history with relevance and personal involvement. Their plan was to introduce the content of the period and then have that content translate into a more applicable and real-life drama. The study began with books, films, art, and other information. Roles for those who would appear at the proposed fair were chosen. There were nobility and peasants, nuns and monks, ladies in waiting, knights, winemakers, crusaders, court jesters, and the inevitable queen. Preparing the presentation of these roles was the next task, as students moved from what they would wear to who they would be and how each person's role would relate to other roles.

The fair was held during the winter, after many hours of student research, study, and preparation. Its high point was the banquet in the Great Hall (the cafeteria), where more than 150 parents and guests entered students' vision of the past. According to the adult team members, "Student commitment . . . was intense and totally internalized; students were making a public declaration of scholarship and cultural appreciation" (Collamore 1988, p. 39).

The teachers said that "the fair was an opportunity to understand the disparities in political, socioeconomic, and technological advancements that are still found in the world today. The Medieval Fair gave our students not only an experience in living history, but also a greater understanding of their place in today's world" (Collamore 1988, p. 40).

The Geography Master Card. "Hey, Mrs. Wallinger, may I please take my geography test?" Does this sound like a typical middle school student? Probably not. But at Bay Minette Middle School in Alabama, the question is repeated often. Students who take and pass the test get a Geography Master Card. The card is a kind of reverse credit card; on it, students save credits rather than charge expenses. The credits are redeemable at the school canteen. Teachers designed the program as an incentive to encourage students to expand their knowledge of the geography of their country, state, and world. It is a voluntary exploratory curricular experience.

The first test is for mastery of the map of the United States. There are maps of other countries and one of the sixty-seven counties of Alabama. Students are asked about their knowledge of the shape of the area and its principal cities. Scoring is simple. Only a perfect score is acceptable for recording. There is no failure for not passing, and tests can be taken again.

According to Robin Rhodes and Florence Strong (1989), teachers at Bay Minette, there has been an additional benefit from the program:

> The faculty has been pleased with the enthusiasm of the students—especially among the traditionally low achievers. It is within this group that the greatest percentage of participation and mastery has occurred.

For example, the percentage of students in this group mastering at least one test is 97% compared to 56% for the average to high achievers who have also mastered one test (p. 45).

The teachers hope to expand and improve the Geography Master Card program. They hope that geographic ignorance will soon be replaced with a genuine understanding and knowledge about the world in which Bay Minette students live.

Are Interdisciplinary Units the Road to the Future?

Lounsbury (1989) has asked, "What will students need to know in the 21st century?" We add another question: "What will students need to be able to do in the 21st century?" Greg Hart (1989), a middle school science teacher in the Bellingham School District in Washington state, suggests that what will be most important to our students will be their attitudes, values, and beliefs. He goes on to say:

> Let's forget math and reading as ends in themselves. Let's move our students toward a sense of stewardship for land and air and water. Let's move them toward a beneficent attitude for one another; a harmony of spirit which will cut through the meanness and cruelty of so many today. Let's develop a nation of geography that begins at home and extends even further abroad. Let's develop an affection for America, for its people, its traditions, its history, its majesty. Let's give our students a sense of purpose by focusing their thoughts and efforts on our most pressing problems (Hart 1989, p. 29).

Judy Sterrett-Pegg, former middle school program consultant for the Volusia County Schools in Florida, has many of the same thoughts about what our students should know and be able to do. She says:

> Since we are unable to know the future and the life that it will hold for each of our students, then we must give them a working knowledge of their history. I do not mean a memorized version but a basic understanding of the major concepts and how to find whatever else is needed. Then the students will need the skills to take on the new challenges of a fast technological information society. Our old method of teaching facts is no longer relevant, since the facts are too numerous to know (1989, p. 37).

In *Turning Points*, the Carnegie Council (1989) makes a most pertinent statement relating to curriculum, exploration, advisement, and the interdisciplinary nature of our world:

The conditions of early adolescence have changed dramatically from previous generations. Today young people enter a society that at once denounces and glorifies sexual promiscuity and the use of illicit drugs. They live in urban neighborhoods and even in some rural towns where the stability of close-knit relationships is rare, where the sense of community that shapes their identity has eroded. They will seek jobs in an economy that will require virtually all workers to think flexibly and creatively as only an elite few were required, and educated, to do in the past (p. 8).

Can interdisciplinary units fill all these needs? At Eastern Kentucky University Laboratory School, Mary Strubbe (1990) explored the usefulness of interdisciplinary units with her students. Her conclusions? When interdisciplinary units are used, students (1) take a more active role; (2) help clarify the effective and ineffective parts of the unit; (3) talk about the units in ways that help validate the experiences in the eyes of parents and the community; and (4) see the interconnectedness of the world around them. In short, what interdisciplinary exploration does is bring more reality into the classroom while broadening the scope of young adolescent thinking.

An interdisciplinary curriculum satisfies many definitions of a good curriculum: curriculum as the sum total of all the curricular and co-curricular experiences of the middle school; curriculum as a means of providing a variety of experiences, programs, practices, and settings; curriculum as a combination of programs that are interdisciplinary in content, exploratory in nature, and cooperative in structure.

Connors and Irvin (1989) find great support for the interdisciplinary curriculum in the middle school:

- 88 percent of the middle schools that were recognized in the government's "schools of excellence" program have exploratories or electives, whereas only 45 percent of the randomly selected schools do.

- 97 percent of the "excellent schools" have clubs and intramurals, whereas only 45 percent of other schools offer them.

- 68 percent of the recognized middle schools have interdisciplinary units planned by academic teachers, whereas only 29 percent of the schools in the random group do.

Edward Barnhart (1987), principal of Vivian M. Sterling Middle School in East Wenatchee, Washington, and a member of the NASSP Committee on Middle Level Education, sums up the need for expanded exploratory courses by saying that such courses help students become interested, interesting people who are more likely to know what to do with their lives. Of course, if limited to only a few courses, the full benefit of such experiences may be lost, but by making exploration a philosophical underpinning of the middle school curriculum, the possibilities are limitless.

Effectively Organizing Time and Space

One stereotype of young adolescents is that they are inattentive, impulsive, and intellectually flighty. This view has evolved in part as a popularized and simplistic expression of adolescence as "a period of storm and stress" as suggested by Hall's classic study of adolescence (Hall 1904). Certainly there are youngsters for whom one or more of these descriptors might be accurate at any given moment. Other youngsters, however, regularly pay attention, complete long-term projects, and pursue absorbing scholarly interests. The point is that every sort and condition of mental accessibility imaginable appears in the middle school population. Decisions about apportioning time for instruction, for individual and small-group work, and for other activities should accommodate as fully as possible the wide variety of learning styles and behaviors characteristic of this developmental period. And teachers should be prepared to help students learn and develop strategies for managing their time.

No single schedule can accommodate the variety described above. Yet a schoolwide structure that accommodates some essential elements has to be created. The challenge becomes one of organizing time and space to accommodate the greatest number of principles and people while ensuring a bare minimum of inflexibilities. Organizing teachers and students into subsets of the community, such as interdisciplinary teams, and assigning those teams to particular wings or sections of the building is a good first step in creating the master schedule.

After inflexible times such as arrival and departure, lunch, and classes taught as off-team teachers have been determined, each team of teachers should take responsibility for working out a team schedule for the time that remains. Because teachers are closest to the instructional program, they are in the best position for establishing instructional priorities and judging the most appropriate way to apportion time. They can recognize opportunities for multidisciplinary instruction, ways to coordinate homework and testing, and strategies for uniform support of curricular initiatives. When the majority of a team's classes are taught by teachers on that team, the teachers involved are in the optimal position for designing curricular plans that, in their informed judgment, best suit the individual and collective dispositions of their students.

The Case for Cooperative Learning

If we want students to be able to function in a cooperative society—indeed, a cooperative world—when they reach adulthood, we need to teach them the skills they will need to do so. Most young adolescents want to be part of a group, so cooperative learning seems to be a natural and promising strategy for helping them learn. The benefits of a full-functioning, cooperative learning program are numerous. Teachers say that they see greater social support among the students and a more positive psychological adjustment to the atmosphere of the middle school. Cooperative learning helps students acquire the collaborative outlook that is so essential in most walks of life (Johnson and Johnson 1989). Just as important, learning how to work in cooperative groups and acquiring related social skills helps students learn more of whatever subject is at hand. Students often have higher achievement, increased retention of content, greater use of higher-level reasoning skills, and higher self-esteem. They also seem to have a more positive attitude toward school and toward teachers (Johnson, Johnson, and Holubec 1988). Cooperative grouping techniques foster an atmosphere of inter-dependence in which members grow to value helping and teamwork in order to achieve group goals. Students further recognize, and learn to appreciate, differences among themselves when they are cooperatively grouped. Such realizations foster understanding and subsequent respect for individual differences in aptitudes, talents, and approaches to tasks—an understanding that is certainly useful in the workplace.

Cooperative learning differs from the more traditional lecture-recitation format in several ways. First, there is the positive interdependence among group members. After the first steps in communication and trust building, students become aware of their responsibility to see that all group members succeed. Also, within their groups, students are aware that they will be held accountable, as individuals, for mastering the assigned materials. Initially, teachers need to take considerable time to help students realize that they are responsible to themselves and to the group and that piggybacking on another's work or success is inappropriate.

Cooperative learning groups are typically heterogeneous in both the ability and personalities of the students, and everyone shares in performing leadership roles. Group members share information and provide help and encouragement to one another. Both the content of the lesson and the social skills needed to be successful in the group are important. Leadership, communication, collaboration, conflict management, and trust are all important aspects of cooperative group work. Several teachers with whom we spoke emphasized that these interpersonal skills need to be specifically taught and not left to chance. They strongly believe that if the time is not taken to develop a sense of "groupness," then cooperative learning becomes little more than small-group assignments in which a designated leader often does the bulk of the work, while the rest of the group gets part of the credit and everyone ends up dissatisfied in one way or another.

Simply stated, cooperative learning combines instruction in social skills in heterogeneous (or sometimes homogeneous) student groups with an emphasis on academic content (Johnson et al. 1988). Anyone who is thinking about using cooperative learning in the classroom needs to be aware that it involves more than arranging students haphazardly at tables where they work on similar lessons and have permission to occasionally socialize. Cooperative learning is students working together to solve the same problems or pursue a common goal.

Ways of Grouping for Cooperative Learning

There are more than a dozen established structures for organizing cooperative groups at the middle level. Some of the most widely used are Jigsaw, Student Teams-Achievement Divisions (STAD), Think-Pair-Share, and Group Investigation. All of these structures spell out social and academic functions so that students learn how to contribute to group goals (Kagan 1989). Teachers who are responsive to their students' need for accomplishment and constructive interactions with peers use these grouping structures liberally, sometimes employing several different structures at once. Using the structures frequently can help students make cooperative skills a natural part of their behavior.

It is not wise for the teacher to always decide who will be in each cooperative group. Young adolescents become increasingly concerned about having some authority over their lives, some freedom to choose what they learn and with whom they do it. Allowing them to choose whom they will work with in the classroom is an immediate and valued manifestation of the concept of "freedom of choice." It further encourages a learning environment that acknowledges individuality and rewards initiative, mutual support, and responsibility—behaviors at work when a group is functioning well.

It may be appropriate to group some students according to what they have already learned in subjects that are highly sequential, such as mathematics. The Joplin Plan, a scheme whereby all students are grouped for mathematics instruction that is offered at the same time, allows limited grouping by achievement (Slavin 1987). This arrangement has produced some qualified academic benefits, and it also satisfies the surface logic for matching students with like abilities. To track students beyond this minimal level, however, is to risk serious damage to self-concept in return for unproven and very limited benefits.

The case for teaching cooperative grouping strategies and techniques at the middle level represents a philosophical point of view that is compatible with the basic tenets of the middle school movement. The key issue is that teachers working in teams must be authorized to make decisions about how their team members are grouped, and they must use the structures that serve their students and their academic goals most fully.

For middle level teachers looking to both capitalize on the developmental nature of the students and provide more active learning experiences, some form of cooperative learning seems made to order. Young adolescents are both eager and in need of learning ways to be more productive members of the social order. They seek situations over which they can have some power and control. They are ready, both affectively and cognitively, to assume greater degrees of responsibility.

Advocating Multicultural Awareness

During the early adolescent years, students become more aware of the many cultural differences among people in both their immediate environment and in the world brought home to them through media. As budding moralists, they naturally make comparisons and wonder why things are. Why do different peoples eat different foods? Why do we speak different languages? Why is poverty more prevalent in some societies?

A trademark of the American educational tradition at its best is the continued celebration of ethnic diversity that constitutes our national heritage. At its worst, our trademark is ethnic and racial conflict that reflects our individual and societal failures. Both the celebration of diversity and an analysis of prejudice have parallels in schools, because the school population reflects the community. Cultural fairs, for example, can celebrate the diverse ethnic groups in a community, state, or region as well around the world.

Teachers who lead their students in explorations of our extraordinarily pluralistic culture create situations that build powerful, reciprocal friendships between generations. *Foxfire* is an impressive example of a program that puts students in touch with the culturally rich life and traditions of Appalachians (Wigginton 1985). Middle level spinoffs of *Foxfire* have spread across the nation (Wigginton 1976). North Carolina teacher Eric Mortensen traveled with his students into the Appalachian culture of the western part of the state. There they got to know a community made up of Cherokee native Americans and the descendants of Scotch-Irish immigrants. They heard stories of the Indian removal via the Trail of Tears. They searched for artifacts on sites of ancient Cherokee hunting grounds, learned about superstitions and the religious beliefs of fundamentalists, copied recipes for 'possum, and grew to appreciate the laconic humor and fascinating stories of these friendly mountain people. Their minds were opened to the richness of contemporary folk customs in a bicultural context that served as a microcosm of multicultural America.

Youngsters' interests are earnest when their cultural education is firsthand, authentic, and concrete. They are curious to know about the day-to-day lives of people in cultural contexts different from their own; they want to know what people eat and what their household routines are like. They enjoy and respond to their music and other arts and crafts, because they can relate to these concrete representations of an unfamiliar culture. Distinctive values and religious beliefs are also a foundation for comparison and reflection that feeds their expanding interest in people's philosophical beliefs. Eric and his students learned a lot about the people in Appalachia; they also developed a deeper kinship among themselves and a new understanding, tolerance, and respect for regional differences among people.

Gerry Rudman and his students from Elm Place Middle School in Highland Park, Illinois, spent a series of long weekends in different ethnic neighborhoods of Chicago, sleeping in church basements or schools and documenting the customs of each neighborhood with camera and notebook in hand. In sharing this adventure, adults and children moved closer together in understanding and compassion for each other, and they acquired a solid experiential foundation for future readings and more conventional social studies treatments of the ethnic communities they visited.

Curiosity about other human beings and their lives never ends. When teachers cultivate their students' natural inquisitiveness by leading them into responsible social inquiries like those described here, they create situations in which they also become learners. They model values and attitudes that are reciprocated by students and benefit everyone.

Integrating the School and Community

A century or more ago, it was common for young adolescents to serve apprenticeships to learn vocations and become an active part of the community. Their perspectives and values were influenced by the adults with whom they interacted. Although no one would likely advocate a full return to that era, many teachers recognize the benefits of that kind of hands-on learning. In fact, most young adolescents *want* to gain knowledge from firsthand experience. Responsive schools today offer opportunities for students to participate in community service activities, so they can bring what they have learned back to the more formal setting of the classroom. Doing things that are useful to others and that are recognized as such is one of the best ways of developing feelings of worth and belonging. Whether the service is reading to young children, tending the town green, or canvassing for a community cause, both students and the community benefit. Schools can take advantage of already existing programs, or they can invent new ways for young adolescents to benefit their community and grow as citizens.

Without active community service, students' only formal exposure to fundamental social values will probably be through short readings and perhaps class discussions of current social issues. Community service fosters active social idealism and responsibility (Lipsitz 1984). It can also give students the opportunity to learn about the democratic process in action. Supervised project team meetings are a good place to let students practice the democratic deliberations and cooperative skills that they will need if they want to participate in the governance of their city, state, or country. A school that offers such opportunities is making an important investment in the mature growth of our citizenry.

A Way to Make a Difference

A major part of the rationale for teachers and young adolescents' organizing themselves and carrying out service work is to show students through firsthand experience that they can make a difference in the world. Helping other people spurs students' moral and ethical development. Students value being recognized for becoming more adult-like and serving as contributing members of their adult-directed community.

In the last decade, a number of prominent educators and national education organizations have promoted the idea of a period of mandated community service as a part of the school curriculum. Such service is still mostly talk, though a few innovative middle schools are finding ways to infuse their exploratory curriculum with an exciting new service orientation. HUGS (Helping Us Grow Through Service and Smiles) is a community service program at the Challenger Middle School in Colorado Springs, Colorado (Andrus and Joiner 1989). Elaine Andrus is the coordinator of the HUGS program, and her enthusiasm for what she calls "service learning" is magnetic. The program is organized to provide all 900 students in the school with a regular opportunity to contribute to their community through service. Each of the nine interdisciplinary grade-level teams at the school adopts at least one community agency or project in the Colorado Springs area. This becomes the team's opportunity to contribute "service and smiles" for the school year.

Students at Challenger are involved in a variety of service projects. Some are part of the "adopt a grandparent" program while others move in the other generational direction to assume "big buddy" roles at a local Head Start program. The Colorado Deaf and Blind School is also one of the groups served. Andrus, in her role as coordinator, acts as a liaison, resource, evaluator, and cheerful advocate for all.

The HUGS program has matured to the point where it is almost an integrated part of the standard curriculum offerings. Andrus says the program has many benefits:

- It provides a special vehicle for creating interdisciplinary theme units.
- It helps students develop caring, critical thinking, decision making, cooperation, and coping skills.
- It help students develop a positive self-concept and enhanced self-esteem.
- It fosters an awareness of the environment, as it relates to personal, social, career, and even academic development.

At its very best, youth service embraces two essential characteristics, reciprocity and reflection, the first of which refers to "the server and those served (who both) teach and learn" (Lewis 1988). In other words, youngsters who give also receive in the form of lessons learned from the beneficiaries of their work. Reflection refers to intentional activities in which youngsters represent their insights and ideas based on the service experience. These activities may take the form of poetry or some other art, or they may be proposals to improve the lot of fellow citizens. When adults and children commit themselves and participate together in good causes, they create bonds that reward both generations.

For example, a student team in one school carried out a project they called "Adopt-A-Business." Individuals and small groups of students "adopted" a business in their small town so they could learn about every aspect of that business. Students served brief apprenticeships and learned basic economic concepts, such as supply and demand and over-head. In the process, they helped the business and themselves. Another team of 6th and 7th graders investigated their town's landfill problem, finding out how much garbage the town produced by sorting different types of refuse in their own homes, weighing it at the end of the week, and extrapolating realistic figures about the volume of types of garbage produced in their community. This was information that had not previously existed, and it helped conceptualize recycling practices that would benefit the town (Stevenson and Carr in press).

In a combination of curricular work and service, a team of 11- and 12-year-olds at the Main Street School in Montpelier, Vermont, investigated Food Pantry, a local agency that provided food relief to needy people in their community. By visiting, interviewing, reading, and gathering information through published materials and local specialists, they prompted increased local attention and developed activist positions on several related issues: hunger at home as well as around the world; gardening sciences, especially pesticides and other chemicals; nutrition education; and the political causes of poverty. The children realized that their group did not have the power to right the wrongs they encountered. But they also realized that through active promotion, they could educate the adults of their community toward more responsible actions on behalf of needy citizens of Montpelier.

Ensuring that students have a variety of experiences in performing services that benefit others puts into action many of the democratic and traditional social values of our interdependent society. Community service is a way to truly teach the social studies curriculum. Historically, schools have left this work to families, churches, or youth groups like the Boy Scouts of America. In a recent five-year period, though, more than 100,000 new service organizations were started (Gibbs 1989). The 1990s should be especially propitious years for students to become active participants in a trend rooted in our national culture.

The ultimate solution to the problem of how to solve basic human and environmental needs not only in our society but beyond will require collaboration involving government, specialists, and common citizens. Now is an opportune time for adults to become unofficial teachers and draw youngsters into serving the community and becoming responsible citizens. In doing so, they will discover the joys of working together for a common cause, and they will see that adolescents truly are ready for meaningful involvement in the community.

■　　■　　■

From setting the climate to using the advisory, from organizing by teams to promoting multicultural awareness, we see evidences of practices reflecting values. When practices reflect values, learning becomes more meaningful. And when learning becomes meaningful, students are well on the road to becoming responsible.

5

Letting Go: Visions of the Middle School Curriculum

Sitting at the back of the room, the observer watched as a group of 8th graders worked through the lengthy test that their teacher gave at the end of each unit. Having glanced furtively backward several times, one of the students finally turned to the observer and said, "This test is stupid."

The observer, supposing this was just another one of those notorious 8th grade behaviors, said nothing.

"This is stupid," the student protested again, this time in a louder voice.

Not wanting to create a scene, the observer whispered, "What's stupid?"

"This," said the student, pushing the test forward.

It was a test like other tests, several pages filled with multiple-choice, matching, and short-answer questions. So the observer said, "It doesn't look stupid. It just looks like the teacher is trying to find out whether you learned what you were supposed to."

"That's what's stupid about it. It's all what the teacher thinks we should know. Why don't they ever want to know what **we** know?"

■ ■ ■

This book tells a compelling story about educators trying to improve the quality of education for early adolescents. It is surely one of the most important stories of this century and one that is certain to continue. Yet if we step back and consider the theoretical framework surrounding the reform of middle level education, the story falls short in one crucial aspect—a broad and considered notion of what ought to be a curriculum for the middle school. The purpose of this chapter is to imagine ways this question might be answered. In doing so, we will first need to understand some of the reasoning that has driven the middle school movement and the kind of change it has encouraged.

The middle school movement has drawn a good deal of its inspiration and momentum from the persistent admonition that good middle schools follow from a clear and sensitive understanding of the characteristics of early adolescents. Many middle schools and state middle level organizations have adopted some variation of the slogan, "In the middle, the kids come first." Yet it has become increasingly clear that this idea has more than one meaning. In the curriculum area, it may lead down at least two paths.

On the first path, the characteristics of early adolescents are seen as traits that are determined by their particular stage of development. For example, popular wisdom has it that early adolescents are characterized by flighty actions, rapidly changing and superficial interests, short attention spans, slavish compliance to peer group norms, and generally "strange" behaviors. Good middle schools are thus usually defined as those in which adults try to adapt institutional arrangements to characteristics like these. Thus, interdisciplinary teams are formed to make policies and procedures less confusing, and to help advisory programs address affective issues, exploratory programs cover technical and aesthetic topics, and activities programs meet personal interests. Furthermore, a premium is placed on teachers who are understanding, on cooperative learning, and on projectlike learning activities. On this path, the improvement of middle level education involves adapting instruction and institutional features to the observed characteristics of early adolescents so as to get them to do what we want them to. Improvement of this kind is like a fishing expedition; it amounts to finding the right bait to put on the hook.

The second path, like the first, begins with the characteristics of early adolescents. Here, however, those characteristics are defined more broadly than in the first line of reasoning. Early adolescents are not seen simply as victims of a developmental stage (for example, as "hormones with feet"), but as people who are experiencing that stage of development and simultaneously living in the world at large. As such, they have important concerns, questions, and issues regarding themselves and that world. They are real human beings in search of expectations and meanings. In part, this view recognizes that so-called developmental stages are largely social constructions that risk a too-narrow definition of the complex and comprehensive lives of those said to be in a particular stage. In this sense, those people may be perceived as trapped within such a stage, subject to culturally induced expectations and seen only in terms of expected behavior.

On the second path, then, early adolescents are regarded as living both in that stage and outside of it as participants in the larger world. The improvement of middle-level education involves creating opportunities and experiences that might enhance students' understanding of self and society in both contexts. Metaphorically, improvement of this kind is an expedition with early adolescents in which we explore possibilities and help them construct meanings.

The First Path: "Adapting" the Middle School

To date, what has passed for curriculum talk in the middle school movement has almost entirely followed the first path. Both the rhetoric and reality of that talk have focused on adapting instruction to the widely popular litany of early adolescent characteristics. Less frequently raised are questions about whether the curriculum as organized and "taught" through adapted instruction is what ought to be the curriculum of the middle school. Whether it is or not, one thing is fairly certain: the middle school curriculum as we know it today is not one that has been deliberately and consciously created out of a broadly conceived notion of what education at that level ought to be about. Rather, it is largely the same planned curriculum that junior high schools inherited from high schools many decades ago. Ironically, it is this very "high school" way of doing things that proponents of the middle school movement claim they do not want to mimic.

In making this case, we do not want to demean progress that middle-level educators have made in trying to make better schools for early adolescents. As the preceding chapters have shown, there is much to celebrate in the positive climate and creative instructional arrangements that have emerged at this level in the past three decades. Today's middle schools are a far cry from Charles Silberman's description of the junior high school as "the wasteland—one is tempted to say cesspool—of American education" (Silberman 1970, p. 324). But among the important questions that the middle school movement has raised, it has failed to press the ultimate issue, "What should the middle school curriculum be?"

Lapsed Memory and Other Curriculum Mysteries

To understand the middle school movement's oversights regarding the curriculum question, we must turn briefly back to the beginnings of the junior high school outlined earlier in this book. Although the first known middle-level-type school appeared in the 1880s, what might be known as the junior high school movement really began around 1910 (Toepfer 1962). The impetus for separating out grades 7-9 from the then popular K-8/9-12 arrangements resulted from several factors (Gruhn and Douglass 1947; Van Til, Vars, and Lounsbury 1961; Kliebard 1986).

First, the majority of young people left school between grades 6 and 8; an earlier introduction of a high school-type curriculum would presumably ensure that those who did drop out would have some introduction to classical subjects. Second, there was an increasing belief that 8th grade was too far to extend elementary education. Third, educators believed that a specialized junior high school, as part of the larger social efficiency movement, would provide a better opportunity to sort students out for future education or work. A fourth reason, though not as powerful as the others, was the call for recognition that preadolescents ought to be kept apart from post-pubescent students on the basis of developmental differences. Finally, in a few of the locations that had begun 7-12 schools, the possibility for a separate junior high school presented a way to relieve overcrowding at the high school level. As Kliebard (1986, p. 125) put it, "The junior high school . . . is one instance where the success of an important educational innovation benefitted by the fact that the ideas of two or more powerful interest groups intersected at that point."

Thus, the reasons for establishing junior high schools had mostly to do with either preparing for or assuming some of the functions of the high school. Theoretically, the passage of laws restricting child labor and extending compulsory schooling by the 1930s should have led to a rethinking of the rationale for and programs of the junior high school. But this was not to happen; for the most part, the junior high school continued to be a junior version of the high school.

Of course, there were other curriculum currents during these years. "Progressive" educational ideas like the child-centered school and the social-problems approach to the curriculum surfaced in junior high circles to form the basis for "problem-centered core" programs. These programs came to be used in blocks of time during the day, and other parts of the day were reserved for separate subjects and activities programs (Gruhn and Douglass 1947; Faunce and Bossing 1951; Hopkins 1955; Southern Association of Colleges and Secondary Schools 1958; Hock and Hill 1960; Van Til, Vars, and Lounsbury 1961). Some theorists suggested extending the spirit of these programs across the whole school (Hopkins 1941, Faunce and Bossing 1951); nevertheless, block-time core programs were found in only about 12 percent of junior high schools by the 1950s (Wright 1958).

This reading of history suggests that the accepted structures of the junior high school helped to cloud memories of why the junior high school got started and thus inhibited rethinking of its purpose and programs as those reasons dissolved under new conditions. A more proactive question, however, is why the new middle school movement of the 1960s overlooked the curriculum question as part of its larger reform agenda, especially as it followed so closely on the heels of the burgeoning, though admittedly small, movement for problem-centered core programs. No doubt this lapse had more than a little to do with the fact that the junior high school, despite rhetoric surrounding it, never escaped the more general rubric of secondary education. And in that context, we should never forget the power of the traditional subject-area approach or its renewed vigor in the shadow of the Sputnik launching in the late 1950s, just as the middle school movement got underway.

The "Absent Presence" of the Curriculum Question

The widely read literature in the early years of the middle school movement pressed hard for a clearer understanding of early adolescence and organizational innovation in those schools (e.g., Eichorn 1966, Grooms 1967, Alexander et al. 1968, Moss 1969). Although curriculum "needs" were often outlined in broad domains of learning, the program of the school was described in terms of separate subjects and mild correlations among them. This view of the curriculum has persisted throughout the movement, with only a handful of exceptions. Most prominent among these were Lounsbury and Vars' (1978) restatement of the case for a problem-centered core program and Stevenson's (1986) description of a curriculum approach based on early adolescents' inquiries into their own concerns. Other writers (e.g., Beane 1975, Arnold 1985, Hargreaves 1986, Beane and Lipka 1987, Brazee 1989) called for similar curriculum reforms, but the curriculum question has remained one of the weaker links in the chain of middle school events.

Yet, as we have seen throughout this book, the middle school movement over the past three decades has involved significant change, not only in theories about middle level education but in actual school practices. No feature has become more clearly associated with the middle school concept than the interdisciplinary team arrangement. It is here that we can look to get a clearer picture of what is presently happening with the middle school curriculum.

Interdisciplinary teaming appeared in middle schools as early as the 1960s. Its primary purpose was to bring together teachers from the four so-called academic subjects to collaborate in decision making while providing a more defined and secure space as early adolescents made the transition from self-contained elementary school classrooms to the highly specialized, subject-centered high school. Less well articulated were the opportunities interdisciplinary teaming offered for correlating and integrating content and skills from the subject areas involved, and the educational benefits such connections offer to early adolescents. Some middle level educators understood these possibilities and worked hard toward them. But their efforts most often dissipated in the press of time constraints, weak support, parental misunderstanding, and the growing clamor for subject-defined content and skills.

Nevertheless, over time, teachers have come to appreciate the collegial interaction of team planning, especially with regard to keeping an eye on students who are experiencing difficulty. However, team members in many schools still struggle over subject-area loyalties that seem to interfere with serious interdisciplinary curriculum arrangements. This local struggle has been further complicated by the press for stricter curriculum mandates and testing programs at the national and state levels. These mandates are almost always defined along traditional subject-area lines. In other words, interdisciplinary teaming has become long on "teaming" but short on "interdisciplinary." As far as concerted efforts at authentic integration are concerned, Vars' (1966) admonition that team teaching may be "the Devil in disguise" has appeared prophetic.

The fact that these teams were (and are) almost always organized around the "big four" academic subjects also meant that other subjects and their bodies of knowledge, like art, music, industrial arts/technology, and home economics, have remained in their historically peripheral positions as "exploratory" or "special" subjects. Recent attempts to find a more inclusive language, like "core" for the academic subjects and "encore" for the rest, suggest a kind of educational "spin control" as teachers of these other subjects continue to find themselves on the edge of the curriculum. This conflict is just one example of how the separate-subjects approach, with the perennial isolation of content and assignment of status among disciplines, continues its stranglehold on the middle school curriculum.

Even theoretical attempts to further the cause of the larger meaning of interdisciplinary education show relatively little progress in breaking down subject-area lines. Such attempts proceed from the assumption that connecting bodies of knowledge amounts to little more than finding out how each subject can contribute to a particular topic (James 1972, Jacobs 1989, Carnegie Council on Adolescent Development 1989). Thus the preeminent position of the separate subjects persists—and though the possibilities for dynamic correlations are limited, genuine integration of knowledge seems almost entirely out of reach.

This critique of interdisciplinary arrangement may seem somewhat odd if one assumes, as in the first line of "adaptation" reasoning we described earlier, that curriculum planning should begin with separate subjects and that simple correlations among them represent genuine curriculum reform. For several reasons, it is time we called that assumption into question again and recognize that it is a problematic one at best (Beane 1990b).

The separate-subject, or disciplinary, approach to the curriculum represents the world of subject-centric academicians and not necessarily the rest of us, including early adolescents. When we come to a puzzling situation in life, do we really ask ourselves, "Which part is mathematics, which science, which social studies, and so on?" Of course not. The fact that the curriculum of schools is organized this way, even in most interdisciplinary arrangements, means that it is an artifice of real life created by academic institutions. For early adolescents, the separate-subject approach presents a fragmented organization of loosely connected information with no coherent sense of unity in learning.

But the artificial nature of the separate-subject approach is not its only problem. As early as the 1940s, emerging evidence suggested that the subject-area approach was relatively ineffective, regardless of claims about its popularity for college preparation (e.g., Aiken 1941, Mickelson 1957). Moreover, the definition of worthwhile content, dominated as it is by classical academic scholars, continues to marginalize knowledge created out of cultures other than that of the white, intellectual (and almost always male) middle class.

Over time, this approach to the curriculum has paralyzed our thinking to the point that a language for describing alternatives is barely visible. Yet we must understand that the subjects themselves, both "academic" and "other," were created more out of political struggles than considered educational reasoning (Tanner and Tanner 1980, Kliebard 1986, Apple 1986, Pokewitz 1987). It is no wonder that calling the separate-subject approach into question today evokes fewer questions about curriculum organization than about conflict with the powerful network of educational elites (text and testing concerns, certification bureaus, academicians, etc.) off of whose symbiotic relations this approach lives.

We believe that the separate-subject approach has failed early adolescents and their schools. Even the subject-area associations themselves are beginning to call for ways to connect their content with other areas through meaningful use of themes (*ASCD Update* 1990). In short, the central problem in the middle school curriculum is the failure of too many middle-level educators, even in some of their most innovative interdisciplinary work, to see beyond the possibility of merely adapting traditional structures like the separate-subject approach to the characteristics of early adolescents.

Unpopular as this kind of critique may be, it is nevertheless necessary if we are to imagine possibilities for a genuine and powerful education for early adolescents. As previous chapters in this book have stated, some middle level educators have made dramatic strides in improving instructional arrangements. However, they only begin to suggest what ought to be the general framework for a middle school curriculum. For that we must first decide what and who middle schools are for.

The Second Path: New Visions of the Middle School Curriculum

Answering the question, "What ought to be the middle school curriculum?" depends partly on our understanding two major—and related—concepts regarding the purpose of the middle school. The first is that the primary and most important clients of the middle school are the early adolescents who attend them. We may recognize that many factors press on the curriculum, including federal and state curriculum mandates, parental and societal expectations, the deep structures of tradition, the interests of subject-area specialists, proposals from within the middle school movement, and the interests of local educators. Each of these is powerful in its own right—and where two or more intersect, the effects seem almost overwhelming. Yet none of them can be as central as the educational interests of the early adolescents for whom these schools are intended in the first place.

The second concept is that the middle school ought to be regarded as a general education school. This means that the middle school should deal with widely shared concerns of early adolescents and the world they live in, rather than the narrow interests of academic or vocational specialization. Early adolescents are young people, still very much in the process of forming a sense of self and social meanings. With few exceptions, they are not in a position to make career decisions; nor are adults to make such decisions for them. Thus a central purpose of the middle school is to help early adolescents to do well at being early adolescents, not simply to prepare individuals for some unpredictable future direction that their lives may take.

The understanding of general education involves the concept that early adolescents, like all of us, are caught up in life as an affective event. That is, the topics that engage our thought and action most fully are those having to do with personal and social questions. The search for self and social meaning makes our lives richer and more satisfying. Moreover, we use and create important knowledge for this purpose, not to lead us into increasingly obscure and mystifying games of academic trivial pursuit.

It is these concepts that guide the second path we described earlier— the possibilities for a genuine middle school curriculum that fully engages early adolescents in the construction of self-knowledge and social meaning. Following are three visions of such a curriculum that have recently been described.

A Middle School Curriculum

Beane (1990a, 1990b) has proposed a new possibility for the middle school curriculum based on the concepts that the educational interests of early adolescents are the central purpose of the middle school and that middle schools are general education schools. The curriculum he describes would begin by discovering the concerns of early adolescents and the world in which they live. To do this, of course, teachers would have to talk with adolescents as a serious part of curriculum planning. Later we describe an example of such planning, but for the moment we can name what some of the concerns are, broadly speaking. For instance, many early adolescents are often concerned about:

- The developmental changes they are experiencing, and trying to understand them.
- Developing a personal identity.
- Questions surrounding values and morals.

- Securing a place of some status in their peer group.
- The maze of adult expectations.
- Their future lives.
- How to deal with commercial pressures.
- Changes in their immediate environment (e.g., family discontinuities) (Arnold 1985; Stevenson 1986; Beane and Lipka 1986, 1987).

Among adolescents' concerns in the larger world are interdependence among peoples; cultural diversity; environmental problems; economic issues such as personal security and the distribution of wealth; the advancing pace of technology; conflict among peoples; how the future might shape up; relations among freedom, power, and responsibility; and the like. Moreover, these concerns or issues are common in that they enter into people's lives regardless of what they do, who they are, where they live, and even though some people may not be explicitly aware of them.

If we examine these two kinds of concerns, we begin to see that, in many cases, they are differences of degree rather than kind. That is, the concerns of early adolescents are most often personal or micro-versions of larger concerns in the world. As shown in Figure 5.1, when the two sets of concerns are aligned in this way, themes begin to emerge at their intersections that connect early adolescents and the larger world.[1] These themes offer rich opportunities for a provocative, compelling, and powerful middle school curriculum and thus ought to be the themes around which that curriculum is organized.

Imagine, for example, a thematic unit on transitions in which early adolescents are engaged in learning about the various changes they are going through as part of their own development—and simultaneously about changes that are taking place in the larger world. In so doing, students may study what change is, how it affects peoples' lives, what leads to it, and the ways in which it actually happens. Imagine a unit on interdependence in which early adolescents examine their own peer-group workings alongside relationships among peoples on a global scale. Here they may look at questions related to status, conflict, cooperation, competition, sharing, cultural diversity, and so on. Picture a unit on wellness in which early adolescents connect their own wellness with environmental concerns on a larger scale as they study pollution, nutrition, disease, stress, conservation, and health regulations.

---

[1]Those familiar with classroom curriculum theory will recognize here the integration of what have been called the "emerging needs" and "social problems" approaches to curriculum organization.

Figure 5.1
Intersections of Personal and Social Concerns

Early Adolescent Concerns	Curriculum Themes	Social Concerns
Understanding personal changes	TRANSITIONS	Living in a changing world
Developing a personal identity	IDENTITIES	Cultural diversity
Finding a place in the group	INTERDEPENDENCE	Global interdependence
Personal fitness	WELLNESS	Environmental protection
Social status	SOCIAL STRUCTURES	Class systems
Dealing with adults	INDEPENDENCE	Human rights
Peer conflict and gangs	CONFLICT RESOLUTION	Global conflict
Commercial pressures	COMMERCIALISM	Effects of media
Questioning authority	JUSTICE	Laws and social customs
Personal friendships	CARING	Social welfare
Living in the schools	INSTITUTIONS	Social institutions

From James A. Beane, *A Middle School Curriculum: From Rhetoric to Reality* (Columbus, Ohio: National Middle School Association, 1990). Used with permission of the National Middle School Association.

If we look more carefully at each of these examples, we begin to see how they offer significant opportunities in the development of knowledge and skill. Each case is potentially knowledge-rich in that it calls forth an array of facts, principles, concepts, and skills from a variety of sources. Each also implies the use of skills related to communicating, problem posing and solving, computing, valuing, and researching. As well, students learn more about developing self-concept; taking social action; and engaging in critical, creative, and reflective thinking. Young adolescents thus learn a variety of personal, social, and technical skills. Each curricular theme also presents many opportunities to bring to life concepts that ostensibly guide our lives, but that are often diminished in the curriculum, namely democracy, human dignity, and cultural diversity (Beane 1990c).

This vision of a middle school curriculum is organized around units whose themes are found at the intersection of early adolescents' concerns about themselves and issues that all of us, including early adolescents, face in the larger world (see Figure 5.2). Obviously, this approach is

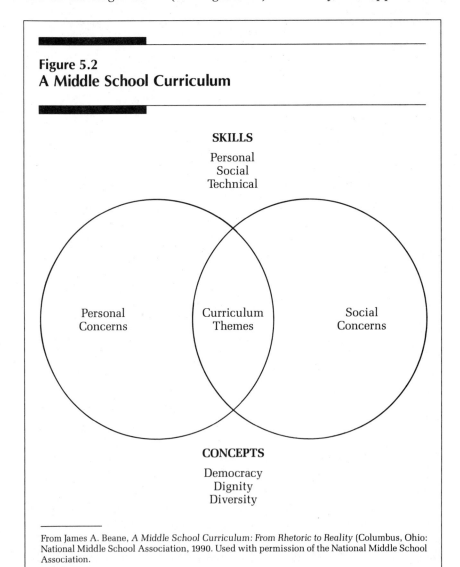

Figure 5.2
A Middle School Curriculum

SKILLS

Personal
Social
Technical

Personal
Concerns

Curriculum
Themes

Social
Concerns

CONCEPTS

Democracy
Dignity
Diversity

From James A. Beane, *A Middle School Curriculum: From Rhetoric to Reality* (Columbus, Ohio: National Middle School Association, 1990. Used with permission of the National Middle School Association.

quite different from current conceptions of the planned curriculum, particularly as it transcends the traditional separate-subject organization. It is also different from some of the progressive problem-centered core programs that found their way into junior high schools in the past. Those were almost always placed in a block of time for part of a day that also included separate-subject programs. We propose that a thematic approach, such as the one Beane describes, should be the whole curriculum and define the entire middle school program, with the exception of some time for young people to participate in activity programs and school governance.

The Middle Level Curriculum Project

One of the most promising attempts to address the middle school curriculum question is the continuing work of a group known as The Middle Level Curriculum Project (McDonough 1991).[2] A network of teachers, administrators, state department personnel, and university professors, this group has been working since the spring of 1990 toward creating a theoretically sound and practically useful conception of the middle school curriculum.

The central concept with which the group is working is that the curriculum ought to be a search for self and social meaning. The sources for such a curriculum are found in three kinds of questions:

1. *Questions early adolescents have about themselves.* These may include questions about self-concept and esteem, future plans, and developmental changes associated with early adolescents as they are personally experienced.

2. *Questions early adolescents have about their world.* These may include questions about the peer group, families, cultures, societies, and the global community, as well as particular conditions in any of them.

3. *Questions that may or may not occur to particular early adolescents, depending on their circumstances, but that are nonetheless posed to all of them because they live in the common world.* These may include any questions regarding issues, problems, or concerns that are commonly faced by people because they live in an interdependent world. Of particular interest here is the fact that these questions exist even though

---

[2]The Middle Level Curriculum Project is currently coordinated out of the School Services Bureau at the University of Wisconsin-Green Bay and is chaired by Lee Mc-Donough.

particular early adolescents may not see them because of geographic location, ethnocentrism, or other factors.

In an effort to clarify these sources of the curriculum, members of the project have asked early adolescents in a variety of settings to identify questions they have about themselves and their world. Responses have been remarkably similar across settings and frequently involve questions about personal attitudes and behaviors, human relations, school policies, family conditions, war and peace, environmental problems, prejudice, poverty, and other significant issues (The Middle Level Curriculum Project 1990). The persistence of questions at that level of significance clearly puts to rest the notion that early adolescents are only concerned about superficial topics and momentary whims.

In addition to exploring possible sources for the curriculum, members of the Middle Level Curriculum Project are also considering what self and social questions might suggest for curriculum organizing centers, what knowledge might be engaged by such questions, and what roles teachers might play in helping early adolescents construct self and social meanings. One probable and helpful outcome of this project will be a description of the group's own work that could suggest how others might think about curriculum planning and development at the middle level.

Rethinking the Curriculum in a Local School

Imagining answers to fundamental questions is often regarded as the theoretical musings of people far removed from everyday life in real schools. But not for the staff of the Cross Keys Middle School in Florrisant, Missouri, who routinely engage productively in this kind of musing. Cross Keys Middle School is a public school with a diverse population, not unlike thousands of other schools. What sets it apart from many is the large imagination of the people who work there.

Having tried many of the common features of middle schools and some rather unusual instructional arrangements, the people at Cross Keys came, a few years ago, to a point where they began to question the curriculum itself. In short, they realized that the way in which the curriculum was organized did not promote meaningful or engaging experiences for early adolescents. In search of other possibilities, they struck upon two key concepts that guide their present efforts.

The first was a realization that the metaphors guiding their teaching were inappropriate—metaphors like the child as empty vessel, or blank tablet, or miniature adult. In place of these common types, a new metaphor was created that is known as "entrancing." This metaphor says that good teaching involves five dimensions: entering the child's world, exploring that world with the child, introducing the child to the adult world, "working" in that world, and searching for meaning (Cross Keys Middle School 1990).

The second key concept involved identifying levels at which teams of teachers might work together. Of the five levels identified, the first four parallel possibilities discovered by many interdisciplinary teams at the middle level: sharing students and time, sharing resources, promoting common skills, and sharing a topic to which each subject area might contribute particular information. However, the fifth level suggests a major break with traditional curriculum organization:

> Teachers agree upon a concept which connects the student' learning and has no content area barriers. Teachers relinquish their areas of content specialization and begin to draw objectives and activities from their wide range of human talents and experiences both in and outside of their formal training and area of certification. Once again, they become human beings, competent and experienced in life itself, first, and in content areas only incidentally (Cross Keys Middle School 1990).

Following from these two concepts, teachers have developed several units around significant themes that encourage early adolescents to search for meanings as they explore their own lives in connection with the larger world. Although much that is included in the planned units is drawn from knowledge traditionally treated within particular subject areas, the units themselves designate no subject-area identifications or teacher roles related to them. The work at Cross Keys is still in progress, but it is already apparent that students have scored at least as well or better on standardized tests of traditional content and skills as have cohorts in previous years.

Schools like Cross Keys are often singled out as models that others might simply adapt in their own schools. This may likely be the case with regard to the thematic units developed at Cross Keys. Mimicry at that level would be unfortunate, however, because the real lesson at schools like Cross Keys is not so much in their curriculum artifacts, but rather in the large struggle they carried out to think about what the curriculum ought to be and the process they used.

Implications for the Curriculum

Although these three visions were developed independently, they have similar implications for what ought to be involved in the middle school curriculum. Some of those implications include the following:

1. The questions and concerns of early adolescents ought to be an explicit source of the curriculum. This requires that teachers plan with young people so that their concerns and views of the world are heard and acted upon. It also means deemphasizing such usual sources of the curriculum as examination content, disciplines of knowledge, next-level expectations, teacher interests, and special-interest expectations like those of business and industry.

2. Organization of the curriculum should extend beyond interdisciplinary approaches that retain subject identities—and move toward alternatives that actually transcend separate subject areas. One example is the use of themes that emerge from the concerns of early adolescents and those found in the larger world.

3. The primary use of knowledge ought to be to help early adolescents search for answers to questions they and the world pose. This means deemphasizing typical uses such as passing examinations, preparing for the next course or level of schooling, preparing for particular occupations, or acquiring some narrowly defined cultural capital.

4. Just as knowledge and skills are not ends in themselves, they ought to be pursued in a functional context in which their use is apparent and worthwhile (Vars 1987). In this way, early adolescents may come to see that knowledge and skills are living dynamics, rather than fixed and abstract objects.

5. Teachers and early adolescents should have more control over the curriculum. The increasing centralization of curriculum planning in state and central office bureaus should be reversed, as in some current restructuring efforts, so that people in local schools have more freedom to plan and carry out new possibilities for the curriculum. In this spirit, the curriculum visions described here are not top-down versions of alternatives to the mandated scope and sequence of subject-centered courses. Instead, they are conceptual descriptions of curriculum possibilities whose forms would be worked out collaboratively in local schools.

6. Curriculum planning should have less to do with narrowly prescribing performance objectives and examination questions, and more to do with posing and clarifying self and social questions; identifying significant organizing themes, activities, and knowledge; and finding resources.

7. Although the curriculum should engage common questions and concerns, it is quite possible, even likely, that all early adolescents might not learn the same particular information. This idea flies in the face of current efforts to name a fixed set of information for all young people, but it more realistically recognizes the ongoing knowledge explosion and

the need for common ways of understanding that may be arrived at through varying informational routes.

8. The definition of who is learning in the school should be expanded to include teachers and other adults who work there. Typically, adults have many of the same questions about themselves as do the early adolescents surveyed by the Middle Level Curriculum Project. Moreover, concerns about the larger world are shared by people of all ages. For this reason, adults cannot simply provide answers to powerful questions, but must seek them along with young people.

9. Along those same lines, the curriculum should be "constructivist," enabling young people to construct their own meanings rather than simply accept those of others. This requires that adults recognize that early adolescents are not adults, and thus may see things through their own lenses.

10. Although the curriculum should obviously be "affect-loaded," it clearly should engage cognitive activity as well. In so doing, it calls for an end to the separation of the two, including the differentiation between academic and affective programs, that still plagues our schools (Beane 1990c).

At the same time, it is important to recognize what these curriculum visions are not. First, they are not anti-intellectual; they do not retreat from either knowledge or skill. Quite the contrary, all offer possibilities for engaging rich and deep knowledge as well as related skills that bring knowledge to life, repositioned in the context of significant questions and concerns. The view here is that knowledge and skills are dynamic, not static, and that their organization into separate disciplines is wasteful and disengaging for early adolescents.[3] The demand for knowledge, including that created within and between disciplines, will be even greater as teachers and early adolescents come together as whole human beings rather than by narrow definitions of subject-area lines.

Second, these curriculum visions are neither whimsical nor superficial, neither simple nor simplistic. There is no suggestion here that teachers ask early adolescents, "What do you want to do today?" or that both simply play with the latest fads. Rather, this view of curriculum proceeds from powerful and significant concerns of early adolescents and the world in which they, and we, live. These young people are no longer defined only by their developmental stage, but as thinking, feeling, and questioning people who also happen to be early adolescents. Like-

---

[3]We suggest that this is actually true for the overwhelming majority of adults as well, who, apart from schools and universities, do not investigate problems or concerns according to subject areas.

wise, their teachers are no longer dull disseminators of information or glitzy instructional gymnasts; instead, they are fully professional guides, helping early adolescents explore their world.

A Case in Point

Advocates of these new visions of the middle school curriculum are often asked to describe what their ideas might look like in practice. The following vignette offers a glimpse of one case that closely matches those visions.

One of the authors recently had an opportunity to work through a thematic unit with a group of early adolescents.[4] Rather than telling the whole story of this unit, we want to focus here on how it was planned. It is possible that the curriculum visions previously described might be read through the lens of the social-problems approach that some teachers use to organize themes for their classrooms. Although this approach presents a compelling alternative to the separate-subject approach, it does not necessarily engage the questions that early adolescents them- selves have—particularly those about the personal side of issues. If we really mean to focus on the concerns of early adolescents, their voices must play a powerful role in a curriculum that addresses both self and social meanings.

■   ■   ■

The group began by developing a list of questions they shared about themselves and their world. Next they looked at possible connections between "self" and "world" questions and the possible themes those connections suggested. Then they reached consensus on a theme for our unit (we settled on "Living in the Future") and planned activities to seek answers to the self and social questions. Along the way, they also identified the knowledge and skills they would need and where they were encountered in their previous school experience.

All of us wanted to know, of course, what it would be like to use this thematic approach and whether it would work. Several things became clear to us as we planned the unit. First, early adolescents

---

[4]This experience, reported by James Beane, was orchestrated by three other teachers: Barbara Brodhagen, James Dunn, and Gary Weilbacher.

have powerful and significant questions. Second, they are capable of seeing connections between personal and larger world concerns, of naming themes, and of selecting topics that deserve group consideration. Third, early adolescents take this work very seriously; we spent several intense hours in planning—enough to exhaust us older people. Fourth, early adolescents are able to identify engaging, worthwhile, and creative activities, as well as the knowledge and skills they need to carry them out. For example, they decided to research family health histories to identify personal, future risk factors; to design a "preferable" community of the future; to survey age-mates at other schools about their desires for and fears about the future; to research past predictions for this decade; and to learn about ways of making personal goals and decisions.

Finally, and perhaps most startlingly, the students easily named the subject areas in which such knowledge and skills might ordinarily be found and where they had previously encountered some of them in school. That is, they understood the curriculum theory behind this project.

Two points consolidate this observation. The first is to report what these young people identified as knowledge and skills they would need to carry out the unit. These included reading, writing, researching, interviewing, problem solving, computation of percentages and ratios, graphing, drawing, listening, estimating, scheduling, photographing, question posing (for surveys and interviews), resource finding, comparing and contrasting, note taking, and using computer skills. They indicated they would need to know more about history, cultures, current events, new technology, health, geography, demographics, anatomy, biology, communications, mathematics, and more. In other words, they demonstrated not only the possibility for engaging integrated content but the need to do so as well.

The second point involves what they had to say about this kind of curriculum organization during a spontaneous question-and-answer period with the school principal. Some quotes are especially illustrative:

Things in school are always separated out. They should be together.

When teachers just tell us what to learn, it doesn't mean anything. They should let us have something to say about it.

We know there are things you want us to do that are important. If only you would do them in a way that was interesting to us.

There might be a set curriculum, but there ought to be different ways of doing it.

[On gifted and talented programs] There are so many activities in this, they can do what they want and go to different levels.

[On coming to school] You know I don't like to come to school. For this I would.

[From a student who is labeled "emotionally disturbed"] They usually make me go to a separate room during this time because people think I am a nobody. Here I am happy. I feel like I am somebody.

Again, these comments were made during a spontaneous conversation with the school principal, not as part of a guided evaluation of our work. In this sense, we were struck not only by the sense of how this curriculum approach might work, but also by the implications the young people saw for institutional aspects of the school.

■　　■　　■

Teachers who have genuinely done this kind of work—the kind that builds from the concerns of young people and their world—will hardly be surprised by these observations. On the other hand, the observations should be reassuring to those who have doubts that this kind of curriculum activity results in poor education or is beyond the reach of early adolescents.

New Curriculum, New Institutional Structures

The institutional structures commonly found in middle schools have formed in relation to the curriculum intentions as, for example, in the case of traditional scheduling with a strict subject approach and block-time scheduling with interdisciplinary teaming. Thus it follows that the kind of curriculum change discussed in this chapter would call for a rethinking of many aspects of the school organization. These changes ought to be worked out in each local school—but we mention some possibilities here.

If we understand that the practice of homogeneous grouping by ability or achievement developed in relation to specialization in the subject-area curriculum, then we should also see how a general education curriculum based on widely shared concerns would involve deliberate use of heterogeneous grouping. Thematic units planned in cooperation with early adolescents necessarily involve a wide range of activities for a whole group and for small groups. In this way, a unit would offer opportunities to explore issues in various ways and to varying degrees of depth. As individual differences are accounted for in the everyday work of the group, such arrangements as gifted and talented and special education programs would no longer be necessary. In fact, a general education curriculum in which democracy and diversity are prized would insist that young people, in all their diversity, be brought together, not separated out.

Teachers would no longer be seen as the holders and disseminators of specialized pieces of information but as guides in the search for self and social meaning. Like the young people with whom they would work, teachers would need to develop skills in problem posing and solving, information finding, and so on. Although teachers might have more or less knowledge in relation to a theme, what is important is that they share a common commitment to working with young people in this way. As they plan and work with any group of early adolescents, they would likely encounter instances where other adults, from the school or community, could offer particular assistance to the group. What this means is that teams of teachers would not necessarily be formed on the basis of prior subject certification, but because they are able to work together well themselves.

In addition to these aspects of teacher and student configurations, others might be called into question. For example, groups of young people might be formed on a multi-age basis; or a group might stay together for all three or four years in the middle school. Teachers might stay with a group for one or more years or for a particular thematic unit or for only parts of one unit.

Because learning would no longer be defined simply as acquiring sets of knowledge or skills, the matter of evaluation and reporting student work would also need rethinking. An obvious possibility would involve a move toward less judgmental and more descriptive evaluation in which the artifacts of various projects and other activities are gathered in portfolio fashion and summarized cooperatively by teachers and students.

Finally, because young people would be actively involved in planning and themes would arise partly out of their own questions about themselves, the ongoing, "regular" curriculum would be responsive to early adolescents' interests and perceived needs. This does not mean that individual adults would no longer help with individual problems as they emerge, but that special arrangements to address affective topics, like advisory programs, might not be as necessary.

These few examples are not meant to exhaust the possibilities for rethinking institutional structures of the middle school. Instead they are intended to give a flavor of what might be involved. However, from these few it should be apparent that a new curriculum may well call into question even those innovative structures that have emerged as middle school educators have continually adapted the school to the character-istics of early adolescents.

Advocating for a New Middle School Curriculum

As the next chapter shows, many aspects of the middle school movement have important implications for the elementary and high schools, as do the new visions of the curriculum described here. In fact, these visions are rooted in general curriculum theory, rather than in specialized dis-cussions about the middle school. They draw from the long history of child-centered work at the elementary level (Dewey 1902, Rugg and Shu-maker 1928) and from ideas that have also been proposed for the high school (Smith, Stanley, and Shores 1950; Lurry and Alberty 1957; Al-berty and Alberty 1962; Beane 1980). And they certainly overlap with some versions of the recent whole-language movement and the emerging reform ideas of subject-area associations already alluded to.

But to wait for those other levels to come to the same degree of reform-mindedness that many middle schools have would only delay this im-portant work and deny the possibility that middle schools could lead the way in curriculum reconstruction. This kind of leadership may be es-pecially appropriate because broader calls for school restructuring, no matter how radical they might otherwise be, have been slow to take up the fundamental curriculum question.

At the same time, middle school people cannot only talk within their own group about new curriculum visions. The move from a specialized, subject-area curriculum to an issue-centered one today is part of a strug-gle that has been taking place in the larger education field for most of this century (Beane 1987). The grounds for the struggle are not just pedagogical, but political as well. Even in the face of compelling evi-dence, educators, like other people, are often reluctant to give up the regularities of their work and the loyalties they have to accustomed structures. So too are many parents apprehensive about any educational changes that they believe might change the ground rules for their plans for their children. And we cannot ignore the fact that the United States is on the threshold of a national curriculum and testing program that would almost certainly harden the categories of traditional subjects.

Therefore, advocating a new middle school curriculum is more than just imagining changes in everyday life in the schools. It involves broad conversations about curriculum possibilities, bold and frank critiques of the curriculum already in place and the political network that supports it, and a well-articulated understanding of what might be expected from a new curriculum. Through all of this, we must be certain to keep the focus on the fact that we are talking about the lives and education of early adolescents and not the special interests of one or another group of adults.

In the end, it is hard to believe that we would not support what these new curriculum visions offer to early adolescents. Here is the opportunity to help these students make closer connections with the world in which they live, to construct powerful meanings around their own concerns and those of the larger world, to integrate self and social interests, to gain a sense of personal and social efficacy, to experience learning as a whole and unified activity, to bring knowledge and skill to life in meaningful ways, and to have richer and fuller lives as early adolescents. Isn't this what we should all want for early adolescents and their middle schools?

6

Middle School Leadership

Kathy Shewey, of Gainesville, Florida, shares her views of a middle school leader:

When I first started teaching, I was involved in a grade 7-12 program, responsible for five "preps" a day. Although I enjoyed working with the students, I really wanted to be in a situation where I felt I was having a greater impact on their future. It was 1969, and movies like To Sir With Love and Up The Down Staircase were popular. Those movies inspired me to try to be a more positive catalyst in the lives of my students. At about that time, my district began to change to the middle school concept. I transferred to the newly organized middle school—and I found my niche. The flexibility of the program and the family approach to teaching allowed me to reach out to my students in a way that I had never been able to before.

Perhaps the reason I have stayed with middle-grade education so long is that I was constantly involved in new challenges regarding young adolescents. In the beginning, a lot of what we were doing was so innovative that it was a challenge just to work within this new system. I was also in an open-space school, and we were all trying to figure out how to adapt to a world without walls. Winning over parents was a challenge throughout my career; I had to let them know what we were doing in the classroom, and also had to translate the middle school concept to them.

There were other challenges, too, such as when I took over as team leader and when I transferred from a rural school to one in the city. There has always been something challenging about middle school.

I think I was chosen as a team leader because I was energetic and I showed a desire to work with the kids beyond the confines of the classroom wall. I was already involved with them in extracurricular projects, and through these things I was able to demonstrate leadership skills that showed the administration that I could handle responsibility and people.

One way I sustained my energy over fifteen years was that I really do like middle school kids. Working with them and finding new ways to reach them has always been exciting for me. Early on, too, I bought into the team-family concept; and I liked working within a group of other middle school teachers. Of course, changing schools and changing environments, plus working on my master's degree, helped me continue to grow and learn.

Throughout my career, I was always looking for more effective ways of reaching and teaching middle school kids. As I learned more about model teachers and innovative programs, I began to have the opportunity to share my experiences with others through staff development and inservice education. This new challenge is exciting because it gives me an even broader mission, toward having a positive impact on the lives of middle school students.

■   ■   ■

John Spindler of Atlanta, Georgia, talks of his leadership in middle school education:

Of prime importance to me, at the beginning of my middle school leadership, was the freedom given to me to create, innovate, and be open to try new ways of doing things in the middle school setting. Administrators in the district office were willing to give me free rein in establishing an exemplary middle school.

My vision of what a middle school should be was determined largely by two factors. First, I had classroom teaching experience in both high school and elementary (K-8) school settings. I was able to observe and be a part of the organizational and instructional strategies designed to meet the needs of students in both levels. My administrative experience in an elementary school provided an additional foundation for a holistic approach to a child's education. In planning for a middle school, I was able to make decisions based on my personal knowledge of the program from which the children came, as well as the program they were projected to enter after completing middle school. Very few middle school educators have had that opportunity. The need for appropriate transitional experiences in the middle of the K-12 continuum was real to me.

The second factor that influenced me was my graduate school experience. Before that, middle school was nothing more than a concept I had vaguely remembered from reading in the professional literature. At the university, I was influenced toward specialization in middle school education because my advisor knew of my background in both secondary and elementary education. Perhaps he also recognized my interest in innovation and my receptiveness to change. His advisement and counseling were important at a pivotal time in my professional life.

My first year as principal of Lincoln Middle School, in Gainesville, Florida, in 1974 can best be described as exhilarating. The challenge of developing a new program and converting an old high school facility was exciting. I had the freedom to design the program; select the staff; and prepare the students, parents, and community for the opening of school. By clearly communicating the mission of the school, I was able to attract the most dedicated and competent professionals who wanted to be part of the team.

These people were not resistant to change, but open to new ideas and innovations. Being a part of an interdisciplinary team, having advisory groups, and having the proper attitude toward teaching young adolescents were not the only prerequisites for employment at Lincoln. I was also intent on having an ungraded, multi-aged-grouped student body, so that I could provide the most flexible and effective system for instruction. Though some faculty members were transferred to Lincoln from other schools in the district because of consolidation, a good majority of the teachers came voluntarily because of the promise of innovation.

It was a major job to sell these ideas to the community, especially to the parents. Students fit into the system easily, but parents were resistant to change and suspicious of anything different from their own experience. In addition, the desegregation plan for our school district involved extensive cross-town busing for racial balance. We inherited a mix of students who had very little experience with integrated schools. We were not only integrating the student body, but also the parent groups. I found out at that time that it was much easier to integrate the students into a school community than it was their parents.

My success in leading a school is probably the result of my willingness to lead by example and to involve staff, students, and parents in the decision-making process. I have always been a believer in the participatory leadership model. When the entire school was administratively operated with a team approach, it was easier for teachers on the individual learning teams to accept the teaming approach. We modeled our positive team member behavior throughout the campus.

The staff bought into these practices because they had a role in determining the practices. My role as principal was significant in generating the enthusiasm and willingness to try these new ideas and making them succeed. As a principal, knowing what I wanted to do and being able to communicate these ideas effectively and enthusiastically were important factors in the success of the school. Enthusiasm was contagious, and it projected a positive atmosphere throughout the campus.

Getting the middle school going in 1974 was quite a challenge, but an even greater challenge was trying to sustain the level of enthusiasm and desire for high-quality performance on the part of the faculty and staff during the late 1970s and early 1980s. Because of our reputation as an early version of a pure middle school model, Lincoln hosted hundreds of visitors each year. This continuous stream of praiseful visitors motivated us to continue to do our best. This was perhaps the best staff development program a principal could have: staff members articulated their philosophy, practices, and commitment to middle-level education to one group of visitors after another. These visitation days sustained and energized us through a period of time when we could have been tempted by complacency.

Many of our successful teachers became team leaders and administrators at Lincoln—and were then promoted to areas of more responsibility at the district level. This caused a need for continual staff development, to prepare new staff members for their roles on the faculty and to maintain the level of commitment to our middle school practices.

Now my role is executive director of middle schools for a growing metropolitan school district. I enjoy the challenge of administering a rapidly expanding middle school program. My perspective now goes beyond the concerns of the building-level administrator to the wide array of activities experienced by district staff members, particularly in the political arena.

I worry about what seems like overregulation and how it might destroy one of the basic components of middle-level education—the flexibility of the program. Across the nation, we are experiencing legislation that dictates programs, organizational patterns, staff utilization, building specifications, and so forth. Funding and accreditation are often tied to this demand for conformity. Middle school principals have a difficult time meeting all these requirements and, at the same time, meeting the needs of the students in the schools and the demands of the community. It is my hope that this tendency to overregulate will pass and that more local autonomy will be given back to the local school district and principals.

I am encouraged that middle-level education is finally getting the public attention it deserves. The recent Carnegie Report will, I hope, serve as a catalyst for increased funding and resources for our schools, and as a reinforcer for those educators and school systems that have been on the cutting edge of middle-level education reform.

■   ■   ■

W.G. "Bill" Anderson of High Point, North Carolina, paints this portrait of his leadership:

In the spring of 1980, the High Point Board of Education adopted recommendations from a long-range study that resulted in the reorganization of grades 6-12. Middle schools with grades 6-8 would replace the junior high, and grade 9 would become a part of the high school. This recommendation, I thought, gave the school systems the long-needed opportunity to correct the most ineffective part of our educational program.

As associate superintendent for instruction and curriculum, I was painfully aware of the weaknesses in this area. I had been unsuccessful in my work with the junior high schools, especially when I tried to replace the high-school-style departmentalized organization with interdisciplinary teams and a block schedule. It was known throughout the system that no one was pleased with the junior high school program.

Student behavior was a problem. There were more suspensions, expulsions, fights, and other disruptive acts at the junior highs than at any other grades. Student attendance was also poorest there. Teachers were unhappy about the situation and extremely negative; principals seemed resigned to struggling through each year. Parents were also displeased. Many affluent parents enrolled their children in private schools for grades 7, 8, and 9 and then brought them back to public schools in the 10th grade. It was a mess.

But, with the middle school, I saw the breakthrough we needed. It fell my responsibility to guide and direct a two-year study to move us to the middle school concept and configuration. This was a challenge I welcomed, but one that also frightened me, because I knew that if we failed, it would be a long time before High Point would have another opportunity to do something positive and good for these middle-level students.

During the summer and fall of 1980, a reorganization plan was developed, calling for an appointment of a middle school task force and an in-depth study of the concept. The plan also included developing a philosophy and objectives and structuring an inservice program for teachers, principals, and the board of education. The importance of understanding the unique needs and characteristics of middle school students was woven into all phases of the study and planning process.

As the task force made progress in its study, I began to see some attitudes change. People who had been very negative and had displayed hopelessness in the junior high setting began to understand what the middle school should be and how it was different from what we had. I became more convinced that we were headed in the right direction. I realized that the longer we studied the middle school program and philosophy, the more support and enthusiasm we generated, because the heart of it was a program constructed around the characteristics of the students to be served. All the components (interdisciplinary teams, block scheduling, teacher-based guidance, exploratory programs, and intramurals) were the building blocks that gave the program structure and strength.

The time was right. As the study moved forward and as decisions were made about the philosophy, purposes, and organizational structure, lukewarm support grew into enthusiastic endorsement. Many people now realized that we could replace the negative, inappropriate aspects of our program with something that would be academically sound and still be a positive force in the lives of these students. This realization served as the driving force in my own work with the task force and the larger school community.

In the spring of 1982, when all this enthusiasm was peaking and all plans were coming together, I realized that we had no way to evaluate the new program or to guarantee its continuance. I was aware of several school systems that had successfully implemented strong middle school programs, only to have them disappear in a few years. I

didn't want that to happen to us, so we designed a teacher survey organized around the essential components of a good middle school
program. We added sections on student behavior and achievement in
reading. We also developed a student survey and a parent survey.

Our strategy was to administer these surveys in March of each year,
and we used the results to examine and improve the program. These
surveys have, in fact, proved to be extremely sensitive to the essential
components of our program. The surveys have helped us not only
maintain the program, but also strengthen it.

Seven years later, in 1989, the middle schools of High Point were
still flourishing. We have seen achievement improve and discipline
problems decrease. Student personal development has been enhanced,
and teacher morale has changed from the lowest in the system to the
highest. Parents are now moving their children from the private schools
to our public middle schools, and each year many systems in North
Carolina and beyond visit us to observe and learn from our experience.

The success story of the middle schools is the highlight of my
career. Knowing that we replaced ineffective programs with those that
are more appropriate and professionally sound is most satisfying. Still,
I worry about maintaining the high level of professional commitment
that is so vital to continued excellence in the middle grades, because I
know how fragile and vulnerable the new middle school is. I am aware
that (as leadership changes, and teacher turnovers occur) the philosophy, concept, and essential components of effective middle schools
can fade and disappear. I hope we have built the base strong enough,
and involved enough people, to ensure the continuation of the excellent
program that we have.

■　■　■

These three middle school leaders have all recently moved on to new
professional and personal opportunities. Each leader has spent years in
middle school education. Each has had an important role in the reorganization of a school district to include middle schools. Each has played a
significant role in the longevity of those middle schools in the district.
All three have had the opportunity to complete those middle school
projects in which they were involved for so many years. All three have
moved on to other challenges, and all have had the opportunity to reflect
at length on their experiences.

In the past two decades, we have worked with dozens of school districts, in nearly all fifty states of the United States, as those systems have moved from one configuration or another to a middle school format. Our experiences have led us to believe that, in virtually every situation where such a reorganization has taken place, the outcomes were a combination of two important factors: situational factors (e.g., size of the district, reasons for the reorganization, socioeconomic status of the students, etc.) and the quality and commitment of the school and district leadership to middle school education. The degree of success that districts experience is a function of the interaction of these two factors.

Both factors are important—perhaps equally so—and they interact and influence each other. Situational components, however, are difficult to influence in any substantial way—certainly not in the length of time during which reorganization typically occurs. For this reason, therefore, we have chosen to put aside any discussion of situational factors and their impact on the effectiveness of middle-level education in any school or system of schools. We concentrate, instead, on those skills we believe are generic to the creation of exemplary middle schools and their continued success.

The preceding vignettes reveal four skills that are necessary for effective middle school leadership. The institution of high-quality middle schools and their continued success depends on the possession of these skills by the leaders involved—at both the central office level and the school. The following are characteristics of effective middle school leaders:

1. Leaders must possess a clear understanding of the characteristics and needs of young adolescents and must translate that understanding into a vision of an appropriately organized and effective middle-level school.

2. They must be able to make recognizable progress toward the realization of that vision by organizing staff members, students, programs, time, and the building in such a way as to create a unique and effective learning environment based on the characteristics of young adolescents.

3. Leaders must understand what tasks need to be accomplished during the reorganization process and possess the skills of "change agentry" necessary to bring those tasks to a successful completion.

4. They must be able to engage the stakeholders (teachers, parents, students, board members, and central office staff) in a process of shared decision making in the continued long-term maintenance and improvement of the school(s).

Vision: Compassion and Understanding for Young Adolescents

A recent study of the long-term survival of high-quality middle school programs (George 1989) determined that one of the two most important factors in that longevity was a heightened sense of mission and the resulting clarity of vision about the nature of the school. In that study, respondents identified the establishment of quality programs, and their continued existence over a long period of time, as resting on a bedrock of a leadership group that understands and demonstrates commitment to the needs of young adolescents. Exemplary programs are never established in the first place without this understanding; continued excellence in the education of young adolescents is impossible, say survey participants, when there is no clarity about or commitment to the needs of the early adolescent age group.

Some participants in the study were convinced that a written philosophical statement based on the nature and needs of the students is the filter through which successful program deliberations must pass. Participants argued that constant reference to this philosophy when making decisions about curriculum, organization, scheduling, and other program components was more important than almost anything else in the preservation of high-quality middle schools. Written documents, of course, are worth very little unless they accurately reflect the degree of school leadership commitment to the needs of young adolescents and the extent to which that commitment is dispersed among the staff members of the school, the district, and its patrons. If, indeed, this student-centered mission is critical to the duration of high-quality programs, then careful selection of school leaders and their involvement in effective staff development programs seem to be crucial activities.

Identifying and selecting such leaders, however, remains a relatively problematic process in many districts. Respondents to the study were emphatic on one point, however: the high school assistant principalship is not necessarily productive as a source of leaders who are able to commit themselves to the education of young adolescents as a comfortable career benchmark. Yet in many school districts, this is the unofficial career mobility route. In some districts it is virtually impossible to arrive at the middle school principalship in any other way (e.g., from the principalship of an elementary school). In George's (1989) study, high school administrative experiences were perceived as less than proper training for middle school leadership, whether or not the candidates had the required natural affinity for middle schoolers.

112

Participants in this survey argued that many candidates for leadership who emerge from the high school assistant principalship may be interested in the middle school primarily for its utility as a professional "roundhouse" that will permit them to return, as quickly as possible, to the high school as principals. Not only is there little to learn in that role, but the training and experience received in the high school may be considerably counterproductive, in terms of producing effective middle school leaders.

High School Versus Elementary School Experience

High school experience is, of course, not an unbreachable barrier to effectiveness at the middle level. In an inquiry into middle school leadership, as perceived by a sample of middle school principals (George 1990a), many respondents were confident about their ability to overcome the limitations of experience at other areas. One stated:

> Although my teaching background was working with high school students, through reading, research, observation, and listening, I was able to come to understand these kids and their needs. Knowing what they will face at the high school also impacted my understanding of their needs (George 1990b).

In this same study, sixteen middle school principals were interviewed during their first year in that role. All were administrators with prior experience at the secondary level; most had been principals of junior high schools. In answering a question about the reasons why they accepted the middle school position, only one talked about the characteristics of the students as having been a factor that attracted him to the post. In addition, these leaders, experienced with older students, expressed their reservations about the maturity levels of 6th graders and the difficulty the students had in adjusting to the middle school, such as using lockers, having many different teachers, and dressing out for physical education. The principals were also concerned about their own ignorance of the curriculum of 6th grade programs. Some admitted that the energy level of these younger students demanded a corresponding level from the principal that they found difficult to supply: the constant movement of the students, the noise—these were things secondary-oriented administrators had to accept, and it was difficult for them to do so.

In this study (George 1990b) of middle school leadership, one principal said that it was possible for a school leader to understand the intellectual needs of a young adolescent without understanding the other aspects of development—social, emotional, physical, and moral. This leader said that such a limited understanding might cause the principal to mistakenly place an exorbitant amount of emphasis on academics at the expense of the important socialization skills and self-concept needs of the preadolescent.

These administrators expressed their doubts about the value of some changes in student activities (e.g., elimination of dances and tackle football) that had come with the middle school. Because successful coaching has, until recently, been one of the few ways in which leaders could demonstrate their readiness for responsibility, many experienced secondary school administrators have an understandable fondness for interscholastic athletic competition. Even though the departure of the 9th graders and the arrival of the 6th graders created a school that was, in effect, one-third younger, many administrators had difficulty saying goodbye to programs and school activities that had been important parts of their lives. Focusing on the needs of younger adolescents and replacing inappropriate programs was not something they could easily do.

The move to middle school almost always means that the school will be composed of students who are substantially younger than the group who had inhabited the school when it was a junior high school. Successful leaders understand that "business as usual" is inappropriate at best, and may actually endanger the health and safety of the students. When athletic programs continue to emphasize tackle football, bodies are much more likely to be damaged, especially because the helmets do not fit well and the pants are too loose. When cheerleading tryouts remain a highly competitive, sometimes psychologically brutal, contest, young hearts can be damaged in a different way. When positive structures like teams and advisory programs fail to be installed because they are perceived as "too elementary," all young adolescents are at risk. Successful middle school leadership is, indeed, based on an understanding of, and a caring for, older children and young adolescents. It is not soft minded to be student centered.

Communicating the Vision

Effective middle school leaders are able to translate their commitment to the development of young adolescents into a vision of the school that is authentically rooted in the needs of those students. Such a vision, at its best, should be convincingly clear, should be possessed by more than the leadership group, should be compelling, and should unblock creativity. The sort of vision that leads to longevity in good middle schools should have the following characteristics:

- Represent shared values.
- Imply risk.
- Lead to growth and development for professionals in the school.
- Lead to further empowerment of those individuals.
- Provide a roadmap for program implementation, evaluation, and revision.

With so much at stake, there is little wonder that discussions of leadership vision and sense of mission receive so much attention in the literature of today's schools.

One school principal described the need to communicate the vision this way:

> In the beginning (six years ago) this skill was highly necessary, with all these groups, to the point where I developed a "stump speech" that could be given to any group at a moment's notice. Now, teachers, parents, [and] central office use our program as a shining star, where before it was a millstone. My job has gotten much easier in this area now because we have developed so many "true believers" (George 1990b).

In a benchmark study of effective middle schools (Lipsitz 1984, p. 167), the author concluded that the leaders of those schools possessed a driving vision that helped everything make sense. "The leaders of these schools are idealogues. They have a vision of what school should be for the age group" (p. 174). Staff members in the exemplary schools she studied had a vision that led to the willingness and ability to adapt all school practices to the individual differences in intellectual, biological, and social maturation of their students. Struck by the centrality of this vision to all that was said and done in these schools, Lipsitz concluded:

> A central weakness in most schools for young adolescents is a widespread failure to reconsider each school practice in terms of developmental needs in order either to incorporate responsibility for meeting them into the school's academic and social goals or to keep them from being barriers to attaining those goals. The four schools in the study begin with an understanding of young adolescent development that is not tangential to but rather helps form the school's central set of purposes. Decisions about governance, curriculum, and school organization, while different in each school, flow from this sensitivity to the age group. Given massive individual differences in development during early adolescence, it is doubtful that a school for the age group could be successful without this sensitivity (p. 168).

Lamenting the general confusion about the purposes of middle school education and the ignorance about the nature of early adolescence as a developmental stage of life, Lipsitz (1984) determined that in the exemplary schools of her study, the staff members "had achieved an unusual clarity about the purposes of intermediate schooling and the students they teach. These schools had reached consensus about primary purpose" (p. 178).

Lipsitz went on to say:

The schools make powerful statements, both in word and in practice, about their purpose. There is little disagreement between what they say they are doing and what they actually do. As a result, everyone can articulate what the schools stand for. School staff, parents, students, and community leaders tend to use the same vocabulary in discussing their school. While this achievement is in part a result of the principal's superb community relations skills, it is also a reflection of clarity of purpose (p. 172).

And finally, Lipsitz concludes:

Most of the principals, three of whom have elementary-school backgrounds, and most of the teachers, identify their schools as more elementary than secondary. Because these are such coherent schools, there is greater consensus about this issue than in most middle schools (p. 173).

School-Level Organization

The most effective middle school leaders in today's schools are able to make recognizable progress toward the realization of their vision in the organization and operation of the school—through the staff they select, the programs they encourage, and the scheduling they facilitate.

Staff Selection

Bringing the vision to reality depends, in a substantial way, in the ability of school leaders to attract and keep the most effective teachers available. One principal expressed it this way:

Staff selection is a critical skill. Principals must select teachers who are, first, child-centered; second, team players; and third, have teaching skills and methods which stress hands-on [experiences], while utilizing a variety of methods. Content knowledge is important, but not as important as those [other actors]. Content can be learned by a teacher; child centeredness and caring disposition [cannot]. Principals must be able to recognize a teacher who has child-centered qualities (George 1990b).

In an environment that exhibits a firm sense of mission and that has an appropriate organization in place, potential candidates for teaching positions can choose and be chosen with a great deal more certainty and commitment. Finding the best ways to select the "right staff" has begun to take on increasing importance for middle school leaders (Carnegie Council 1989). Targeted selection processes, structured interviews, and other devices are just now beginning to appear on the scene. Most of today's leaders must, however, still rely on their ability to articulate the vision for the school and their intuitive sense of whether the teacher has that elusive "child-centeredness."

Program Development

Capable leaders of today's middle schools understand the organizational implications of the vision of an exemplary middle school. Curriculum is important, and effective instruction is essential. It must be said, however, that even the best middle schools have not distinguished themselves in these areas. In fact, attempts to make significant changes in the curriculum and instructional activities of middle schools, in the first two decades of their existence (1960s and 1970s), foundered on the rocks of inadequate attention to school organization. In doing so, we believe, forward movement in middle school education, especially in curriculum and instruction, was delayed until educators in various places began to realize the central importance of school organization and its power to influence every aspect of a young adolescent's education.

In the early years of middle school development, many educators were caught up in the spirit of the times—and a consuming focus on the individual. Consequently, methods of instruction that focused on the individual and curriculum designs that encouraged individualized learning paths were the rage. Middle school educators, deeply concerned with the characteristics and needs of their students, were naturally fascinated by the appeal of such innovations. Believing as they did, that earlier schools had ignored the students and the characteristics and needs that set those students apart, middle school educators welcomed the individualization movement and wanted their new middle schools to reflect those emphases.

In many districts, therefore, staff development efforts aimed at supporting the move to middle school focused on attempts to provide teachers with the skills to design individualized learning programs and the ability to deliver those programs with teaching strategies that emphasized individualized instruction. Well intentioned as they were, unfortunately, these efforts resulted in extremely limited changes. In many middle schools organized in the years from 1970 to 1980, teachers left staff development programs prepared to teach in ways that conflicted with their own preferences for instruction. New strategies were quickly discarded when they failed to work immediately or when they required additional increments of planning time from harried teachers coping with the stresses of the times (e.g., school desegregation, changing enrollments, etc.). New curriculum designs, packaged attractively, were just as quickly placed on shelves, where they languished untouched for years.

At times, these attempts to change the content of what was placed before the learners, and the methods of teaching that accompanied them, were placed in new open-space buildings designed to facilitate these innovations (George 1975). The hope was that open spaces (also much less expensive to construct in days of booming enrollments) would permit teachers to work together more effectively and would allow learners to work independently under the supervision of instructors. Teachers working together to plan learning experiences for students to work alone is an intriguing concept.

In most places, the consensus that was instantaneously reached by teachers—and maintained firmly until the present time—was that open-space buildings were disastrously poor facilities for teaching and learning. Portable barriers of all kinds were immediately erected; permanent walls followed as soon as teachers could influence decision makers to have them constructed. By the end of the 1970s, open spaces for learning had been walled up, and innovative designs for curriculum and instruction had been packed up—apparent casualties of the "back to basics" movement. Actually, these innovations were as much the victims of educators' failure to recognize the incredible importance of organizational issues and to develop an organizational strategy built on the unique nature of young adolescents. Consequently, we have devoted much attention to these concepts in our earlier discussions of organizational issues.

Effective Scheduling

The master schedule must be designed to make the essential components happen in the school. With the complexity of a fully functioning middle school program, many leaders believe quite rightly that effective scheduling is the sine qua non of the exemplary middle school. They say that without that skill, all of the other efforts to design and implement a quality program will be for naught. Developing a master schedule requires both the courage to try something new and different and the sense of humor to bear the slings and arrows that are flung from those who must live with the inevitable imperfections of any design.

In many schools, quiet priorities sometimes confound the best attempts to establish a polished product at master scheduling time. Some classes, called singletons, are offered only once a day, to one group in the school—and these singletons have to be built into the curriculum. These classes may include journalism, French, Algebra 1, gifted groups, and concert band. The more singletons, the more serious conflicts may develop in the scheduling process. When instrumental music or some other important activity dominates the scheduling process, it may yield groups of students on teams without the sort of demographic balance essential to success.

Here is where the school philosophy and the priorities that flow from it can be severely tested. In most school situations, where official priorities and traditional emphases may compete for space in the schedule, a great deal of final twisting and turning of time is usually done at the end of the entire process, by hand, for each individual student. The final product then becomes the rough draft for the next year.

Critical Tasks of District Reorganization

Concepts of school leadership emerging from studies of effective schools indicate that the most effective school leaders possess three skills (George 1983). First, they are capable of shaping a vision of the school. Second, they are able to articulate that vision in such a way that others in the school subscribe to it. Third, they are capable of making recognizable progress toward that vision. It is this third area, progress toward the vision, that concerns us here.

Hundreds of school districts have reorganized their grade-level configurations over the past twenty years. Some of these change projects have resulted in middle schools with sustained high-quality programs. In many other districts, high-quality programs were either never established or, once established, began to erode so that few traces of those change efforts now remain, save for the changes in grade levels that accomplished other purposes for the district and were thus sustained for other reasons. The difference in these two experiences has a great deal to do, we believe, with the degree of understanding and skill with which the reorganization effort was managed.

Hundreds of additional school districts appear primed to launch reorganization efforts or are ready to install authentic middle school components in existing middle-level schools. We believe that many important tasks must be accomplished in this process. We offer the following "laundry list" as a relatively complete catalogue of decisions that must be made during a district-level reorganization. These decisions are also related to the recommendations of groups such as the National Middle School Association and the Carnegie Council on Adolescent Development.

Such decisions will be made most knowledgeably and implemented most effectively when the involvement by stakeholders is as complete as possible. Involvement is the key. Our experience has been that the process works best when a strategic planning model is followed carefully, including the in-depth and continuing involvement of the district superintendent, board members, parents, teachers, and other school building leaders, as well as outside consultants. A steering committee representing these groups and smaller task groups for each assignment should study and develop a consensus—and a carefully written plan—on these important issues:

1. District Middle School Philosophy

- What do we believe about the characteristics and needs of our young adolescent students?
- What do we believe about schools that are responsive to the needs of such students?
- To what degree are the district guidelines to be interpreted flexibly by individual schools?

2. Organization of Teachers and Students for Learning

- How important is subject specialization in the way we organize our teachers to deliver instruction?
- How many subjects should our teachers teach?
- How important is the teacher-student relationship in our schools? How much time should the same teacher and student(s) spend together each day? Is it important for the same group of teachers and students to stay together for more than one year?

■ When we balance these two factors (subject specialization and teacher-student relationships), what sort of interdisciplinary team organization does it imply for our schools? Will we have grade-level teams? school-within-school, student-teacher progression?

3. Curriculum

■ What should be the nature of the required daily curriculum we offer to our middle school students? What should be required?
■ What optional curriculum opportunities should be available in the form of exploratory, unified arts, or elective classes? What role should choice play here?

4. Co-curriculum

■ How can we arrange for an exciting array of activities in which all students can experience success?
■ What policies will ensure that middle school activities will be appropriate for young adolescents, and that high school activities and experiences will be saved for high school?

5. Advisory Programs

■ How can we design the school so that every student will have at least one supportive adult in the school?
■ How can we ensure that such a program will have the support of all members of the school and community?

6. Instruction

■ What instructional strategies are most appropriate and effective for the education of young adolescents?
■ What methods of grouping for instruction will we arrange for our students' classes? What mix of heterogeneous and homogeneous grouping is best for our schools?

7. Schedule

- How should we arrange the time for learning?
- What roles will be played, in the scheduling process, by the principal, the teacher teams, the central office—and, most notably, the computer services?

8. Leadership

- What will be the roles and responsibilities of various school leaders: team leaders, subject area coordinators, and committee chairs?
- How will such persons be chosen and supported?
- What model of collaborative administrator-teacher decision making will be established in our middle schools?

9. Special Programs

- How will we ensure that the needs of exceptional students will be addressed in the new middle schools? Can such efforts be coordinated with the new model of interdisciplinary team organization?
- How will programs like those for gifted and talented, foreign language, and Chapter 1 students be accommodated in the new program?

10. Staffing and Staff Development

- What sort of career mobility plan can the district establish to ensure that the new middle schools are staffed by the administrators and teachers most appropriate for that assignment? How can we ensure that staff members have informed opportunities for making career choices that may involve moving from one school or school level to another?
- What training opportunities must be designed to ensure that the staff possesses the appropriate knowledge, skills, and attitudes for launching and maintaining the new middle schools? What special training experiences will be required in:
  a. knowledge of the characteristics of young adolescents;
  b. effective classroom strategies;
  c. working on and with interdisciplinary teams;
  d. acting as an advisor; and
  e. being a part of collaborative decision-making groups?

11. Adjustments and Modifications to Buildings and Other Programs

The implementation of middle schools is not simply a middle-level project. All students in the district will be critically affected by the reorganization effort. In one stroke, virtually all of the schools in the district will become "younger." The elementary school will lose the older students, the middle level will be one-third younger, and the high school will be 25 percent younger. Every administrator, teacher, student, and parent in the district will be involved. "Business as usual" at any level—considering the younger populations—will court disaster. Task groups must be formed to respond to the following questions:

■ What communications tactics will be pursued to inform both the internal and external publics of the purposes and programs associated with middle-level reorganization? How will teachers and administrators at the elementary and high school levels be informed and involved? How will parents and community members be informed?

■ What program adjustments will be necessary for the elementary and high schools in the district? How will the members of high school staffs be involved in preparing for the arrival of 9th graders?

■ What adjustments will need to be made to school buildings, at all three levels, to accommodate the new middle school programs and the effects that new groups of students will have on high schools?

12. Evaluation

■ What strategies must be pursued and what data collected for a formative evaluation of the middle school program?

■ What outcomes of the reorganization should be measured for a summative evaluation of the degree to which the middle school program has improved students' education in the district?

Shared Decision Making

Many school leaders have stated that if teams are to work well in a school, a principal has to be comfortable with consensus decision making. The real decisions have to be made at the team level. A principal must have the flexibility to allow decision making to be done outside the office—and must be able to engage in a collaborative process with the staff that results in the school's ability to respond effectively and continuously to the demand for school improvement. Shared decision making promotes personal ownership of the change process, involves collaboration that goes beyond "advisory councils," produces altered educational roles, and improves communication.

Personal Ownership

Organizational systems theorists have long known that there is a close connection between widespread individual involvement in change and personal ownership of the change effort (Weisbord 1987). The more people are involved in responsible and meaningful ways, the more likely they are to support the results of that involvement over a long period of time. This contrasts with their being merely passive observers, or worse, pawns in the process. This knowledge has important implications for middle school leadership.

In the study of program longevity among high-quality middle schools, George (1989) determined that a formal shared decision-making process, necessary for continuous school improvement, was at the top of the list of factors contributing to survival. Participants in the survey emphasized the importance of widespread involvement in the development of policies and decisions that occurred before the new schools opened and in the years that followed. Establishing an authentic faculty-administrator collaborative unit is essential. Policies regarding the design of teams, advisory programs, curriculum, schedules, and building organization are too vital to be left in the realm of unilateral decision making located in the administrators' suite. Not that an administrator's vision is not important, but involving the staff is the way to bring the vision to reality.

Collaboration and Consensus

Shared decision making means authentic collaboration and consensus. It goes far beyond a consultation process, such as the traditional "faculty advisory council" where faculties express their opinions and administrators make the decisions. High-quality middle schools, we believe, emerge from and are sustained by collaborative groups representing all stakeholders in a school.

The need for this sort of collaboration, accomplished through an open and somewhat democratically operated council of peers, does not end with the opening of the new school. Indeed, such a group may make its most important contributions to the life of the school long after opening day. No complex, sophisticated, and successful program for the education of young adolescents can last very long, apparently, without continuing collaboration among faculty and administrators. A regular, often weekly, meeting, usually lasting for several hours, is near the norm for the participants in the survey (George 1989). School districts must, therefore, find ways of identifying leaders who not only have an exalted vision of the school, but who understand that faculty involvement is the way to make significant, long-term progress toward realizing and sustaining that vision.

Altered Roles

Expanding roles increases responsibility. The respondents to George's survey stressed the need for expanding the number of responsible leadership positions within the school following the transition to the new program. At one time, many educators seem to have believed that with the move to the interdisciplinary team organization, subject-oriented departments were no longer needed. Some believed that departments had to be eliminated, or teams could never function fully. The consensus reported by George (1989) emphasizes the priority of the interdisciplinary team as the central decision-making group among the faculty and administration, but adds that departmental concerns also need attention.

In schools where quality programs last longest, department functions are not eliminated, but altered. Titles and responsibilities change so that the person who coordinates social studies, for example, may be called a vertical committee chair, or the social studies curriculum coordinator. These committee chair roles, in long-lived middle schools, turn out to be much more limited than in traditional junior high schools. Stipends and released time are more often allocated to team leaders rather than department chairs. Duties of the subject-area coordinators are restricted to the needs of a particular subject area within the major components of the school curriculum. They may assess needs and order materials, and they may coordinate testing programs. But subject-area coordinators do not have major responsibilities, or budgets, in schoolwide policies, decisions, or programs.

Most schools have coordinators in all major curriculum areas. Typically, these include groups that meet monthly, or every six weeks, in the following areas: social studies, mathematics, language arts, science, reading, physical education, exceptional education, and unified arts.

Other committees may operate in the areas of testing or student activities.

The major importance of these revised quasi-departmental roles may, in fact, be in their utility as training experiences for those who eventually become leaders of houses or interdisciplinary teams. More often than not, team leaders serve in these more limited capacities before moving on to the team function. Filling these second-tier positions virtually doubles the number of leadership roles for staff members to occupy, radically enlarging the group of people who have a stake in the school as a whole.

Many districts have also discovered that serving as a team leader facilitates further professional growth of the sort that encourages the assumption of leadership roles like assistant principal, central office staff person, and principal (Spindler and George 1984). As young leaders gain experience and realize their leadership potential, faculty members develop upward, professional mobility and envision more challenging personal and professional goals. Participation, then, has important staff development potential, in addition to its centrality to the governance of the school.

In some middle schools, the process of shared decision making includes involvement in a variety of committee assignments; and every teacher is expected to serve on at least one committee. Committee work, in addition to accomplishing important tasks for the school, provides excellent training in the knowledge, attitudes, and skills that staff members must possess to effectively contribute to the shared decision-making process. One middle school known to the authors operated the following standing committees during the year: Advisor-Advisee, Social, Articulation (K-12), Instructional Improvement, Library/Media, Staff Development, Public Relations, School Climate, and Lounge.

Improved Communication

Shared decision making of the sort we advocate here has the added benefit of promoting communication and staff awareness of what is happening elsewhere in the school. Schools and other "loosely coupled systems" are often characterized by difficulty in communicating effectively across the faculty and staff. Shared decision-making processes connect separate teams and houses (schools-within-schools), facilitate communications between interdisciplinary groups and subject-matter specialists, and bridge the gap between the regular classroom and the needs of exceptional educators and their students. The formal shared decision-making process goes far beyond the communication possible through office and departmental memos and the sort of information available in conventional, large faculty meetings. These processes therefore create an increased sense of community and promote a growing sense of efficacy among the members of the staff, all of which adds to general school effectiveness.

The Program Improvement Council

In the middle schools of Alachua County, Florida, a formal model of shared decision making, in place for the past twenty years, contributes greatly to the long-term survival of high-quality middle schools in that district. Developed as a part of the change from junior high to middle school in that district, the model that was implemented in the early '70s persists to the present, identified then and now as the Program Improvement Council (PIC). Originally a part of the Kettering Foundation's program for Individually Guided Education (IGE), the IGE decision-making model designed for use in the elementary school was successfully adapted for use in the six middle schools of the district.

The effectiveness of PICs in Alachua County and elsewhere has always depended of the skill and commitment of the school leadership. There have, of course, been lengthy periods over the years when the leaders in an individual school have simply not understood the value of shared decision making or possessed the skill to make it work well. The model has functioned effectively here for long enough, however, to be considered a viable model adaptable for use elsewhere. Hence, we describe it in some detail.

Membership and Attendance

The PIC is a schoolwide policy-making, decision-making, and problem-solving group that brings together members of the faculty, administration, and sometimes parents and students in authentically shared governance. Regular members in a middle school include, first, the leaders of each interdisciplinary team, then the members of the administrative team, a counselor, and representatives from physical education, exceptional education, and the exploratory curriculum. In all, about a dozen of the school staff comprise the PIC.

In addition to the regular members of the group, the meeting is "in the sunshine." In Florida, public groups are required and have a tradition specifying that important meetings be open to the public or, in this case, to the entire school community. PIC meetings are held in a convenient public space in the school (often the library), rather than an administrator's office, a sign that the meetings are truly open to all.

Any staff member can attend any PIC meeting, for any of several, important reasons. Anyone wishing to observe the process may attend. New staff members are especially welcome because attending PIC meetings is a good way to see quickly the essence of the staff's values and catch glimpses of the philosophy that is the driving force of the school. Any member of the staff, as well as students and parents, may attend to speak in favor or against a particular action being considered. However, only regular members may vote. Everyone is aware that PIC is where important decisions are made and influential policies developed.

Mission

The mission of the PIC is to deal with schoolwide issues of many kinds. The effectiveness of the process depends, in part, on how carefully the mission is clarified. Policies that are negotiable are known. The range of problems that can be addressed is accepted by its members. The arena in which its decisions have validity is carefully circumscribed.

The group knows, from the beginning, that many issues and operations are beyond its concerns. The limits of its authority are unequivocal. The group will not deal with problems that focus on a single team or a single component of the curriculum unless those issues have important schoolwide implications. The group will not attempt to alter, set aside, or otherwise attempt to manage state or school district mandates; but they may discuss and take action on ways in which those mandates are met within the school. The school group does not deal with the performance appraisal of individual teachers or with other purely administrative prerogatives. The PIC would not attempt to operate the school in the sense of building the master schedule or taking the first crack at the annual school budget. Nor would the members of the PIC group attempt to solve the sort of daily issues that are more appropriately dealt with by individual teachers, teams, counselors, or school administrators.

In PIC schools, some important concepts are nonnegotiable. Among them are the interdisciplinary team organization, advisory programs, and the commitment to the effective education of young adolescents. The PIC group may discuss problems with those programs or modifications of them—but whether the school is organized into interdisciplinary teams, for example, is not debated. The size, location, and responsibilities of the teams may be modified. The length and frequency of the advisory program sessions may be investigated, but the existence of the advisory program has never been an issue.

Issues and Agendas

Topics that will appear on the agenda for a PIC meeting are developed collaboratively. Often a tentative agenda for the upcoming meeting will be placed in a special spot in, say, the faculty lounge. Any teacher can add an item to the tentative agenda there, or individuals may communicate concerns they have to their team leaders for consideration at the meeting. The final agenda is most often designed by the school administrator; but it is influenced significantly by the concerns and interests of other professionals in the school. The degree of authenticity that can be ascribed to the shared decision-making process is a function of the extent to which the agenda for the PIC meetings actually matches the real concerns of the staff of the school as a whole.

The agenda items from one actual meeting of such a group included:

1. Plans for a visitation from out-of-state educators.
2. Districtwide middle school evaluation.
3. Achieving better coordination of field trips: involving teachers of the gifted, specific learning disabilities, physical education, and exploratory curriculums.
4. Decisions about what to do with "merit school" funds from the state department of education.
5. Intramural playoff regulations.
6. Applications for attending the NMSA annual conference.
7. A brief presentation by a T-shirt retailer.

This agenda is a good example of the way in which fundamental decisions about the nature of the school—and the funds that support it—are mixed in with what might almost be considered trivial items. At one time during the year, the group may debate important philosophical issues concerned with tracking and ability grouping; and at the same meeting, they might discuss whether advisory groups will be permitted to have parties the day before the break for the winter holidays. In another session, the members of the PIC may provide feedback to the scheduling committee before developing the new master schedule for the next year; later in the meeting, they may review testing schedules for the week immediately ahead. Planning for special projects; discussions of how to improve efforts to meet the needs of individual students; scheduling strategies; concerns such as excessive tardiness, report cards, or improving the quality of parent conferences—all are common items for the PIC.

Agendas arise from the continuing policies, problems, and issues that concern the staff, students, and parents of the school. It is important, say those with experience, to attend to the more immediate situational concerns—while allowing adequate time to present dreams and visions that pave the way for change and innovation or to discuss the return to programs and priorities that may have faded or weakened.

Examples of the Team Approach

The PIC group is the school team. It is an interdisciplinary group that shares the same students, the building, the same resources, the same master schedule. Together, the members plan and guide the program for the school as a whole. With important allowances for the skill and commitment of the principal, the school becomes and remains what the PIC decides it will be.

At Trickum Middle School, in Lilburn, Georgia, a Management Team model has been in place since 1984. Members include the principal and the assistant principal, an instructional lead teacher, and grade-level chairs, as well as the counselor, media specialist, advisory council representative, special education chair, and a representative of the exploratory areas. As in many other such teams, members are chosen by the groups they represent, each serving for one school year, each having one vote (including the principal).

At Trickum, the Management Team meets once a month, for an eight-hour day. At least two hours of the meeting are devoted to the development of leadership skills and the sense of unity needed by such a group. The remainder of the time is spent on needs of the school. Each area reports, with events, questions, and concerns.

The principal serves as chairperson of the Management Team at Trickum.

> The team recognizes the principal's responsibility as instructional leader of the school and that the final decision is his. However, the principal recognizes the input of the team as being representative of the school personnel at all levels and strives to use wise judgment in the execution of his responsibilities (M. Moody, personal communication, January 1988).

In the Dade County Public Schools in Miami, Florida, school-based management has been implemented on a broad, perhaps more comprehensive, scale in elementary, middle, and high schools. Though the process is still in a developmental stage in Miami (and in other school districts far from south Florida, like Rochester, New York, and Hammond, Indiana), the emerging model bears a strong resemblance to shared decision-making processes already in place in successful middle schools across the United States. There is much to be learned from a careful study of the evolution of these essentially democratic processes.

Initially in Dade County, school staff members had to undergo an extensive application process, including the involvement of community members, and a vote of the faculty as to whether they wished the school to become involved in school-based management. The teachers' association, the United Teachers of Dade (UTD), took part in developing and instituting the process in separate school buildings in the district.

At Campbell Drive Middle School, shared decision making developed along the lines of the PIC, with important adaptations to the Dade County environment. Members of the PIC group included representatives of the administrative staff, team leaders, department chairs, the parent-teacher group, and student government. Other members were representatives of UTD the migrant office, and any other interested people in the community. Other schools in the district, at the elementary and high school levels, are using a similar process.

The aims of the Campbell Drive PIC are to:

1. Assist school management in organizing the school agenda.

2. Aid in making decisions relative to budget and all other aspects of management.

3. Objectively and effectively serve as a vehicle of communication for all staff.

4. Help management establish an educational environment conducive to increased student and teacher productivity and performance.

5. Assist in the formulation of educational goals and devise a mechanism to measure accountability for achieving agreed-on standards.

6. Promote the team approach in program delivery.

7. Be an advocate for the middle school student and the inherent differences involved.

In the following vignette, Principal Onetha Gilliard tells how it all happened at Campbell Drive Middle School.

■　　■　　■

After receiving the confirmation that our school had been chosen as one of the thirty-three pilot schools to initiate school-based manage-

ment and shared decision making, I attended a staff development exercise on effective schools. The main speaker was an outstanding school superintendent from New York. The first thing he said was that he didn't believe in decisions by committee and couldn't go along with our new headline, "School-Based Management/Shared Decision Making."

Well, my reaction was—and is today—that times have changed, and an organization that changes with shifts in population or economic constraints requires creativity. This can only be met and accomplished with cooperation, trust, brainpower, and mutual respect. Together, teachers, students, parents, and the entire school as a team can form an effective governing cadre to determine the school's needs and possible outcomes.

In my third year as principal, I welcomed an opportunity to experience shared decision making and accountability. Even though we had been functioning in a similar situation, we had never come to the term shared decision making, nor had we actively invited parents to join our weekly meetings. Now, on some occasions, as many as two parents and three students attend and take an active part in the meetings.

Our governing cadre is called the Program Improvement Council (PIC). During our regular meetings, each agenda item is explained by the staff member, parent, or student who submitted the item. It is the individual's ability to persuade the council that determines either defeat or acceptance of the proposed item. If you have the ability to do research, organize a presentation, and be part preacher, then your job is done—sometimes.

At Campbell Drive Middle School, each staff member has an equal voice in our school operation. There is absolute democracy, with one vote per member, providing you were in attendance at the previous meeting. There is no veto power by the principal: I have the same one vote as every other PIC member.

Shared decision making affords staff, students, and parents the greatest opportunity to share in creativity and productivity. Ultimately, I am still accountable for the problems, concerns, and resolutions shared by all. Do I ever want to revert to a non-school-based management style? No! We are operating in a style that creates mutual ownership and accountability.

With so many parts necessary for an effective middle school, it is imperative to empower those in the school to accomplish the task. I believe that empowerment of staff actually gives the principal more power, flexibility, creativity, and freedom to conquer any task, because there is a sense of ownership. With the empowerment of staff, there must be mutual trust, respect, acceptance, open communication, and a sense of being a winner.

Many changes have occurred at our school since the institution of the shared decision-making process. The staff decided to change the number of periods in the school day from six to seven, implement an advisory program, open an interdisciplinary math and science laboratory, and alter the beginning and ending times of the school day. On the other hand, some proposals, such as remodeling certain offices and initiating a student-teacher progression model, have failed to be implemented because they were rejected by the members of the PIC.

■ ■ ■

Middle school leadership is an exceedingly complex, difficult, and life-consuming professional challenge. It has been described by many practitioners as a "splendid agony." We believe that the best middle school leaders will have an even different vision of the school of the future. They will have the capacity to persuade others of the validity of that vision and the ability to make and sustain recognizable progress toward that vision through the use of shared decision making and related skills. These skills are necessary for middle school leaders in the '90s and beyond.

7

Beyond the Middle School

At Arapahoe High School in Littleton, Colorado (not too far from Elaine Andrus and the service learning model at Challenger Middle School discussed in Chapter 4), Principal Ron Booth speaks with enthusiasm about the community service learning experiences at his school. Following a period of study of the needs of local high school students, a school district/citizen's group concluded that the white, upper-middle-class youth at Arapahoe were not armed with sufficient real-life experiences, that kids in their suburban community needed to learn about life outside the classroom.

Consequently, thirty hours of community service is now a graduation requirement at Arapahoe High School. The program, called "Students Out Serving" (SOS), requires high school sophomores to perform fifteen hours of service and complete their experience with another fifteen hours in their junior year. Ninth graders were excluded because it was believed that one more change in their lives might make adjustment to high school that much more difficult. Seniors were not included, so that program planners could judge just how much carryover there might be to real, voluntary community service that year.

Although the program is required and carries no monetary reward for graduation, students choose their own types of community service—and they have made creative choices. As Ron Booth says, students have gone "far beyond candy stripers and delivering Christmas dinners."

For example, some students have worked with the ski patrol in the nearby mountains. Other students have served on the high school campus, signing for students with hearing impairments. Another group of students assists other Arapahoe students with disabilities. Students in this group take students with disabilities to school dances, including helping them get ready in their homes (washing and dressing them, if necessary), driving them to the function, and then driving them home afterward. Another group works in an after-school program at a local elementary school, where many students had been returning to empty houses while the parent or parents worked. The students engage the kids in games and activities until the parents come for them.

So far, the SOS program appears to have had many beneficial effects at Arapahoe High. Booth believes that it has helped the students develop patience, especially those who have been working with young children, students with disabilities, or elderly people. He says that the program helps integrate academic experiences and life skills such as extemporaneous speaking, time management, organizational skills, and socialization beyond the narrow confines of a particular peer group. SOS has provided school staff members with a tremendous new avenue for recognizing students—especially those who are not already successful in academics or athletics. Further, SOS develops a positive reaction among community members who are the recipients of such creative service efforts.

■　　■　　■

As this example shows, the middle school movement, in both philosophy and practice, is going beyond middle schools to emerge in some innovative elementary and high schools as well. This chapter describes such pioneering schools across the United States.

Beyond to the High School

In May 1988, Gene Maeroff, senior fellow at the Carnegie Foundation for the Advancement of Teaching, presented a poignantly persuasive argument that high schools, especially those in the inner city, must become more like elementary schools. Detailing the dismal failure of our urban high schools, Maeroff called for the implementation of a totally different philosophy of education, with the cornerstone being "smaller learning units," much like those recommended by the Carnegie Council on Adolescent Development (1989; see Chapter 1) and implemented in many effective middle schools. He wrote:

> High schools in the inner city must become more like elementary schools, preferring supportive environments that bolster the confidence of students. Experts repeatedly reaffirm the merits of smallness, and yet urban high schools remain Goliaths, as though there were virtue in bigness. Urban high schools must insinuate themselves into the lives of students in ways that make the schools places where students want to be. The schools present themselves to students not as places where they can work toward a better "tomorrow," but as places where they can create a better "today" (Maeroff 1988, p. 638).

By building community among students, the school may foster the values essential for both personal and academic success. Students should help set the rules of the community and participate in its upkeep, as they do in Japanese schools and in some American boarding schools. Activities involving groups of students and teachers would promote bonding, enabling students to feel that they belong to the school and the school belongs to them.

The middle school model has a great deal of promise for high schools, including those beyond the inner city. Indeed, Maeroff's prescription for reorganizing the inner city high school reads like a description of the middle school interdisciplinary team organization and advisory programs:

> A high school of 200 to 300 students with a faculty of its own that is shared with no other school—even though schools may coexist on separate floors of the same building—can be an intimate institution in which students see the same small cadre of teachers over and over again. Time must be built into the schedule for teachers to meet regularly for several hours a week with small groups of students to talk about life and its problems. More effort must be made to inform the adults at home about what students are studying, so that the adults will take more interest in what is occurring in the classroom (Maeroff 1988, p. 638).

In fact, many school districts around the nation have already begun to incorporate modern middle school organizational concepts into their high schools. For a variety of reasons, high school educators have begun to emphasize smaller learning units. Sometimes the district staff has learned the value of such units from middle schools in the district or elsewhere. In other situations, high school educators have recognized, without outside prompting, that older adolescents can also benefit from a more interdisciplinary approach to the curriculum. Some teachers and administrators have arrived at spontaneous decisions to reorganize the high school after using a school improvement process (combining school-based management and shared decision making), which has suggested the need for more "smallness within bigness" as a pathway for improvements in classroom management, dropout reduction, and other problems.

Shared Decision Making at All Levels

Saturn Base

Shared decision making, so natural at the middle school, works at other levels, too. At Little River Elementary School in Miami, Florida, the shared decision-making process is based on the same principles, but organized slightly differently, because of the organizational structure of the elementary school. The decision-making group (called "Saturn Base") consists of six grade-level chairpersons, a chairperson representing all special area teachers, a union representative, and an administrative representative. Members are elected, from their area, by secret ballot. Each of the nine Saturn Base members has one vote. The Saturn Base chairperson is elected from the faculty at large, to avoid conflict. Meetings are open to all members of the staff, although only elected members may vote—except in special cases where another representative of a group is invited to make a special presentation.

At Little River Elementary School, representatives of any group can submit that group's issues and concerns to Saturn Base. Issues might include budget, curriculum, staffing, discipline, and matters that cannot be settled at other group meetings. It is the duty of the representatives to present the concerns of their group and report back to the group.

In the past two years, members of Saturn Base have dealt with many issues. They have proposed, investigated, and initiated several innovative projects, including a restructuring of the kindergarten program, an integrated language arts program, and a "Parent Teaching Center" within the school, where parents take an active role in teaching their own children.

In Saturn Base, the majority rules—and decisions "will not be over-ruled by the principal except for good cause and with the concurrence of the union steward" (F. Zerlin, personal communication, April 1989). In such circumstances, the principal must report to the members of Saturn Base, or the total staff, to explain the reason for overruling the decision, even in the case of emergency decisions. The staff clearly has labored to develop a model of truly shared decision making. As they expressed it:

> We have worked hard to be truly representative of the whole faculty, and this has caused some delays in decision making. When a decision was needed and a vote was to be taken, some representatives wanted to discuss the matter more fully with their grade groups before committing their grade group to a decision. This necessitated delays before a decision could be reached. We have tried to take a middle road on this—some decisions we felt had to wait until grade groups were consulted, while others could be voted on at the meeting with the understanding that the grade group had empowered their grade chairperson to represent them

The faculty, as a whole, is enthusiastic about shared decision making at Little River. They comment:

> We have learned to look beyond the interests of our own classroom and to look at the school as a whole. Staff participation is growing, as individual teachers find their opinions are needed and are valued. When we started [shared decision making], we were careful to limit it to a workable model and workable projects. We wanted very much to succeed. We felt if we succeeded this first year we could add on and grow. There is also the feeling that nothing is written in stone, and if something does not work, it can be changed. Our advice, therefore, would be to start slowly and learn as your model evolves. Hands-on experience is the best teacher!

School Improvement Process

Other school districts have received a great deal of attention for their innovative efforts in the shared decision-making process. In 1982, Hammond High School in Hammond, Indiana, became one of the first schools to become involved in what is known in Hammond as the "School Improvement Process" (Dickson and Knarr 1989). The process eventually came to include all elementary, middle, and high schools in the district—and central to that process is shared decision making. As expressed in Hammond:

A central axiom underlying the importance of the use of this process is that people affected by decisions should have a share in making those decisions. A further axiom . . . is that educational programs and practices which work most effectively are those in which the persons responsible for carrying out these programs and practices actually feel ownership for these same programs and practices (Dickson and Knarr 1989, p. 2.)

These axioms are embedded in the shared decision-making, school improvement process in Hammond, as specified in the master contract between the board of education and the Hammond Teachers' Federation. Decisions at the school level, if they depart from the contract, must be made on a consensus basis, using a modified Delphi technique; small groups discuss the proposed changes, determine trial periods, and gather evidence that will be used to determine the success of the project or plan. A systemwide Review Council has oversight responsibility, coming into play when specific school-based decisions appear to conflict with state or federal laws or regulations.

School-Based Planning Teams

In Rochester, New York, perhaps the most dramatic departures from school business as usual have received a great deal of attention in the public news media and in the professional literature. Significantly higher salaries combined with a substantial increase in accountability for outcomes has made Rochester a district to watch. In the array of new and challenging initiatives underway, the shared decision-making process is, again, at the heart of it all. As School Superintendent Peter McWalters put it:

Teachers will participate in the governance of schools and help set standards for their profession, as well as hold responsibility for delivery of instruction. Principals, in addition to managing the work of schools, will demonstrate a new form of leadership characterized by ability to build collaboration and consensus, and to create a climate of innovation in schools (McWalters 1989, p. 10).

In Rochester, all schools, K-12, are now incorporating these new roles for teachers and principals in what are called School-Based Planning Teams. Each school forms a team consisting of the principal, the principal's designees, parents (up to three), students (at the high school level), and a number of teachers determined by "adding one to the total number of all other members selected for the team." Other members may be chosen by consensus of the members of the team. Each group chooses its own representatives to the planning team.

In Rochester, educators have taken pains to ensure that such groups are more than advisory in nature: they are deliberative, decision-making bodies. This is done while simultaneously affirming that the school principal retains both the authority and responsibility for managing the school on a daily basis and for creating an environment that supports instruction. The principal serves as chair of the planning team, and the team is empowered to act on behalf of the school when their decisions and actions are arrived at by consensus (City School District 1988).

One unusual dimension of the shared decision-making process in Rochester, at all levels, is the factor of accountability. In effect, the superintendent and the school board have raised salaries to previously unheard of levels and have delivered astonishing autonomy to the schools: in exchange, the schools must accept "full responsibility" for the progress their students make against the standards set by the school board. For example, at the high school level, school-based, shared decision making is to be used as the lever to accomplish the graduation of higher proportions of students, as indicated by this criterion:

> A 50 percent increase in the proportion of students who graduate with a diploma of Regents standard graduating class of 1992—current 9th graders [in 1988] (McWalters 1989, p. 14).

Accountability for the middle schools in Rochester was expressed this way:

> [There is to be] an increase in the number of students prepared for academic work of Regents standard in high school. The benchmark goal for middle schools is to deliver to District high schools a 9th grade class in which 60 percent of students qualify for Regents placement. This goal represents an increase of approximately 50 percent over the current placement standard. Middle schools will also show increased success as indicated in high school teachers' responses to surveys of their satisfaction with the preparation demonstrated by entering 9th graders (McWalters 1989, p. 14).

Similar standards have been set for both the primary and the intermediate levels of the elementary schools. The superintendent made it clear, however, that these improved academic standards, and those for middle and high schools, were

> by no means the only expectations that we have for our organization over the next three years. The benchmarks I have established, however, will

provide direction to school planning teams, and serve as a basis for coordination of the efforts of elementary, middle, and high schools in the District's four sectors (McWalters 1989, p. 15).

Even the staunchest middle school advocate would hesitate to claim that shared decision making originated in or is the exclusive possession of middle schools. We argue here, however, that shared decision making has been a hallmark of quality middle school education for the past two decades and has proven to be essential to developing and maintaining high-quality middle schools throughout the past twenty years. We maintain that the process, refined through its use in the formative years of middle school education, has emerged in improved forms useful at all levels of public education.

Division Organization

At brand-new Florin High School, in the Elk Grove School District, near Sacramento, California, Principal William Huyett is euphoric as he describes the shared decision-making process operating in the high school—and in all the other schools in the district. Decisions, policies, and problems at Florin High are addressed through a carefully designed committee system, combined with a "Division" organization. Says Huyett, "Some of our ideas have come out of a middle school concept" (personal communication, 1989).

First, at Florin, the faculty is currently organized into four curriculum divisions that go far beyond the narrower confines of the traditional department setup. The divisions are composed of related subject areas: world cultures and literature; mathematics, science, and technology; visual and performing arts; and health and physical education. In its first year of operation, the school contained only 9th and 10th graders; but the plans were to add 11th and 12th graders in two years, along with a fifth division, American culture and literature. (See "Interdisciplinary Connections" later in this chapter for a further discussion of the Florin curriculum.) For decision-making purposes, at the school level, each division elects a representative to the school Planning Committee.

Along with the division representatives, the Planning Committee has representatives from each of the other standing committees that are a part of the school's governing structure. Such committees include curriculum and instruction; school environment (including physical, social, and intellectual concerns); home-school relations: and, "incredibly important," says William Huyett, the monitoring and evaluation committee. Each sends a representative to the school Planning Committee.

The Planning Committee also has representatives from students, parents, noninstructional staff, and the school administration. It meets several times a month, as do all committees; and meeting times are scheduled in advance and posted on the school calendar.

Huyett says that one reason the process works so beautifully is that all committee members, virtually all the staff, have received effective and appropriate training in shared decision making, collaboration, and other group process skills. "All of us were tired of going to poorly run meetings," Huyett says. Each committee is staffed by faculty members and administrators who have been trained to play different roles in the committee process: one is a leader (a "convener" who does the work of developing the agenda and otherwise preparing for the meetings; often an administrator); and another is a facilitator (runs the meetings; never an administrator).

However the shared decision-making process is organized, and from whatever origins, it performs what is essentially a problem-solving function. Knowledge and ability in the group problem-solving process are essential to the success of a Program Improvement Council concept, or to any other model of shared decision making. A standardized, systematic, and accepted "problem-solving process serves as a framework for effective schoolwide shared decision making, "allowing for creative and intuitive insights as well as incorporating the experiences and backgrounds of those involved in the process" (Marshall 1986, p. 65).

We believe that, too often, school leaders at all three levels, who would otherwise be eager to involve the staff in shared decision making and collaborative problem solving, are blocked by their own lack of skills in the process. Collaborative problem solving, lamentably, is not usually part of the preparation program of today's school administrators. If they were armed with such a structure, all participants in the shared decision-making process, at all levels of schooling, could proceed with more confidence.

Strategic Planning at All Levels: Incorporating Middle School Concepts

High School Futures

Under the leadership of Gordon Cawelti (1989), ASCD has helped high schools move in these directions. In ASCD's third High School Futures Consortium, the application of principles of school organization through the strategic planning process resulted in dramatic plans for reorganization of the high school, along lines familiar to middle school educators. For example, in Bedford, New York, faculty members at the high school are attempting to develop a school-within-a-school model for their 9th graders. The new high school organization "will feature smaller classes, interdisciplinary teaming, and community service to assure smoother transition for students at this level" (Cawelti 1989, p. 32).

It may not be entirely a coincidence that this same district is the location of the Fox Lane Middle School, recognized nationally as a pioneer in modern middle school education. In the early 1960s, Fox Lane, led by Principal Neil P. Atkins (who eventually became an executive director of ASCD) was moving forward with efforts to insert a unique transitional program into the middle of the K-12 continuum (Alexander, Williams, Compton, Hines, and Prescott 1968). The new high school program for the 9th grade was to smooth the transition from middle school to high school and increase the effectiveness of educational processes for that year of high school.

Plans for the reorganization of the 9th grade in high schools are also currently underway in dozens, perhaps hundreds, of U.S. school districts. In High Point, North Carolina, for example, planners are investigating ways to extend the interdisciplinary team organization into not only the 9th but the 10th grade of the district's high schools. Committees are at work in seven different areas of potential change at the high school level: organization and personnel, program and curriculum, advisory programs, student activities and involvement, climate, facilities, and alternative education programs for high school youth. According to a High Point central office staff member, Elsie Groover-Leak, the presence of effective middle school programs already in place has apparently prompted district planners to explore the extension of successful components of these programs to the high schools (personal communication, December 1989).

The Littky-Thayer Story

This story begins with one particularly successful school that embodies most of the exemplary qualities we have described: the Shoreham-Wading River Middle School in New York—and its founding principal, Dennis Littky (Lipsitz 1984, Maeroff 1990). Littky began at Shoreham-Wading River in 1973 with an inspired vision of a school that would balance its responsibilities for students' academic development with activities and organizational designs that would complement youngsters' personal developmental needs. Littky's enthusiasm and energy in meet-ing these goals was infectious, and teacher-colleagues shared his com-mitment to bring about a new kind of schooling. Advisories, interdisci-plinary teams, community service projects, experiential learning, and exploratory curriculum projects proliferated, becoming hallmarks that have established Shoreham-Wading River as a model of responsive mid-dle-level education.

After five years, Littky moved to New Hampshire for a change of pace and lifestyle that included writing about his work in schools. Serving in the state legislature and launching a community newspaper taught him about his new home of Winchester, an economically depressed com-munity of fewer than 4,000 residents. Their 7-12 school, Thayer High School, had also fallen on hard times in recent years. Student attrition, poor academic performance, and discipline problems rivalled the social and educational impoverishment Littky had encountered earlier in his career in the Ocean Hill-Brownsville section of New York City. Thayer was a project urgently in need of a restructuring that a succession of previous principals had been unable to accomplish. Littky applied for the vacant principal's position.

The remarkable story of Thayer's turnaround and subsequent rapid emergence as a model school in the Coalition of Essential Schools is well known in the East. The school's metamorphosis not only produced dramatic changes in students' attitudes about themselves and the im-portance of their education, but it also brought new energies and a more optimistic outlook to much of the Winchester community. Despite the multiple successes of the school, however, some contrary-minded com-munity members resisted Littky's innovations; and a series of hotly con-tested elections and litigation ensued. The urgent importance of clear communication within a community where school practices are evolving successfully but rapidly provides a fascinating, optimistic example of progress in American education (Kammeraad-Campbell 1989).

What may be less well known in the Littky-Thayer story is the central role provided by middle school organizational designs Littky had estab-lished successfully at Shoreham-Wading River. He recognized from the beginning the necessity for all students—regardless of their ages—to experience a feeling of belonging to their school, the other people in it, and its programs. Immediately upon his appointment as the new prin-cipal, Littky went to work observing the school, sizing up more precisely its conditions and needs. Throughout the summer, he met individually with teachers and students, seeking their priorities and communicating his own. Cleaning and cosmetic restoration prepared the building for student-made decorations that would define it as a place where they could make personal investments and feel respected and connected. Steadily, the school was reconceptualized to organize teachers and students into teams, provide advisory groups for every high school student, establish apprenticeships in the community to capitalize on experiential opportunities, and create innovative curriculums that would simultaneously teach fundamental skills and build pride.

An example of combining several of these elements into an interdisciplinary approach is "Dovetail," a team of fifty 10th, 11th, and 12th graders. Interested students were interviewed for the program, and they were promised that they could move through their studies at individual rates while working on a variety of appealing curriculum projects: an archaeological dig, constructing a post-and-beam building on school property, owning and operating businesses, and serving apprenticeships during school hours in local businesses and services. Everyone on the team participated in publishing *Shavings*, a newsletter that would keep the community informed about the team.

The Littky-Thayer story demonstrates clearly that a school design that responds to the human nature and needs of its most immediate constituents can turn around even the most depressed circumstances. Littky and his vision were essential to sustaining the reform in Winchester, of course—but the work he and his colleagues did and continue to do should hearten those of us who are similarly visionary, but more timid about pursuing such ideals. Particularly noteworthy are the middle school values and designs that enhanced their progress. Although the Thayer story is particularly dramatic, it is not the only example of successful application of middle school designs.

Districtwide Innovations

Tom Moeller, assistant superintendent for instruction in Kirkwood, Missouri, is justifiably proud of his school system, which has a well-deserved reputation for excellence in education at all levels. Nevertheless, and perhaps even because of that degree of excellence, in the spring of 1987, the district staff undertook a comprehensive strategic planning process to ensure high-quality education for the year 2000. The process, which began at Kirkwood High School, was designed to be collaborative and participatory—shared decision making of the broadest sort (T. Moeller, personal communication, December 1989).

A design was established to receive input from all administrators in the district, all staff members at Kirkwood High, students, and community representatives. Brainstorming sessions, held separately and confidentially with each group, established how individuals from all of these groups viewed the high school and how it could become "the best high school in the country" in three to five years. A subcommittee then synthesized the agreed-upon items and developed parameters for study. Then a committee of forty-two teachers, administrators, parents, and students looked at these parameters for an entire school year, eventually forming three additional committees (curriculum, student support and readiness for life, and staff development and institutional climate) for developing the high school of the future in Kirkwood.

These three committees conducted in-depth research in their areas, reporting regularly to all staff members. During the spring of 1988, committee representatives traveled throughout the United States to visit programs that seemed promising. Four areas emerged as priorities for the "new" Kirkwood High School: advisor-advisee programs, learner outcomes, transition from the middle school, and integration of the curriculum.

At the beginning of the 1988-89 school year, Kirkwood High began to implement the results of all the deliberations, planning, and workshops that focused on these four areas. The first initiative was the pilot 9th Grade Co-op Team.

9th Grade Co-op Team. The co-op team is an interdisciplinary team based on the middle school program in the Kirkwood school district. After two years, the program has been judged to be unusually successful.

The teachers at Kirkwood High School believed that the success of the program by the end of the first year was worth not only continuation but expansion for the next school year. The teachers witnessed growth in student knowledge, documented through increased homework completion and improved semester grades. They also observed improved socialization skills and enhanced student self-esteem as a result of the group and individual activities. Attendance levels increased following the constant phone and letter communications to parents from the co-op teachers. Many students from the pilot program have talked about how much it has helped prepare them for their sophomore year.

According to Tom Moeller:

> The teachers involved both this year and last year, a total of eight, volunteered for the co-op and were very excited about the possibilities for extending the program to include the entire 9th grade class. We are constantly evaluating the program and making changes where appropriate. Our overall goal [for the co-op program] is to eventually create a 9th grade center that provides for a positive academic and social transition

for 9th graders into the high school environment. We are also beginning to break down the subject matter barriers to help foster the creation of more interdisciplinary approaches to teaching. The utilization of community services has also begun in the co-op teams this year, with continued exploration into further possibilities of this concept in other grades (personal communication, December 1989).

Summer conferences at Kirkwood were scheduled to discuss with the students and their parents their thoughts about what high school would be like, as well as to set academic and social goals for each year. These long-range goals were supported by the establishment of a 9th grade advisory program for the 1989-90 school year. Moeller describes this program:

All 9th graders [at the high school] were assigned to an advisor for the entire year. Instead of having a seventh hour, the students have advisement. The advisors were inserviced this past summer in preparation for the program. A curriculum guide was also developed to help guide them through areas they were not familiar with, such as self-esteem, peer pressure, goal setting, and study skills. Each hour has from two to five advisor groups so that they can work as individual groups or as teams. Each team [of advisory groups] has been assigned a counselor who works with them monthly. We also have a counselor who teaches study skills to all the advisement groups and helps the advisors follow through with the students on the study skills process (personal communication, December 1989).

Flexible Scheduling. Like most high schools, Kirkwood High operated for many years on a six-period day. During the 1989-90 school year, the staff is piloting a second innovation—a "more flexibly scheduled daily schedule," based on seven periods, and offering three optional schedules. One schedule is a conventional seven-period day similar to what one finds in many middle schools. The other two options are block schedules. Each of the block schedules is structured in eighty-seven-minute segments, allowing for more flexibility in planning for instruction in science, home economics, art, American studies, and the co-op team. To our knowledge, this creative option is a rare item in contemporary American high schools.

Contact Period. A third program at Kirkwood High, the "contact period," has been revised and improved. The contact period is designed to "allow students to meet with individual teachers for support or additional assistance" (Moeller, personal communication, December 1989).

This time is placed in the middle of the day, between fourth and fifth periods and paired with lunch. Students use some of their time to eat lunch and the remainder, whenever necessary, to make contact with their teachers. The schedule is arranged so that it is possible for students to see all their teachers. It seems to us that such a program can be a great addition to the newly established advisory program there.

Learning Lab. A fourth innovation at Kirkwood High School takes the place of the traditional high school study hall. Here, faculty members have implemented a "learning lab" concept. Students who once had an undirected study hall are offered the opportunity to obtain assistance directly from teachers in art, math, science, social studies, foreign language, and English. Faculty members also developed a computer lab, where students can work on word processing and data processing. They set up an IBM lab, an Apple lab, and a writing lab, which are supported by the English and business education teachers. As Moeller sees it:

> What this all means is that the students who are assigned to a study block have the opportunity to seek out individual help from each of their academic areas, go to the library, see their resource room teachers, or explore guidance activities in the guidance centers, such as college and career selection, or discuss individual schedules. We tried to provide an opportunity for our students to use a resource that was never in place at the high school before.

Elementary School Programs. In the five elementary schools of Kirkwood School District R7, a similar strategic planning process has culminated in a range of exciting new programs. First, an uninterrupted block of time was set aside for language arts and reading, a period of time that will permit a more holistic approach to teaching these subjects. A new "push-in" program has been implemented to reduce the number of pull-out programs; and the district is at work implementing a co-teaching model, permitting teachers of exceptional students to work in the regular classroom alongside the general education teacher.

At the upper elementary levels (grades 3-5) in Kirkwood, the focus is on an interdisciplinary team model, permitting teachers to specialize in areas of their particular subject strengths and interests. Because students in these interdisciplinary programs would necessarily have more than one teacher, a homeroom concept was implemented to provide each student with a teacher to whom the student could relate, and begin and end the day with. In addition, the time was increased for involvement in art, music, and physical education. Planners recognized, perhaps as a result of their successful middle school program, that teachers working in an interdisciplinary team need a common planning time. Consequently, they built into their elementary schedule a common planning time for teachers at each grade level so that they can plan for their students and provide for integration in the curriculum.

Not surprisingly, the Kirkwood elementary schools are currently studying several other middle school-style options, including the potential for an advisor-advisee program. Also on the study agenda is the concept of multigrade-level teaming, which educators there hope will fit in well with the advisor-advisee program and will enable students and teachers to know each other better. These teaming efforts include the broadening of the base of specialists for social studies, science, and health; the concept of integration of curriculum, as well as compacting curriculum; and the expansion and refinement of the gifted and enrichment programs.

Vertical Teams. In addition to these innovations, the Kirkwood school district has been involved with a grant from the Danforth Foundation, piloting a process known there as the "Vertical Team." Vertical teams are formed to address school improvement, collegiality, individualized professional growth plans, and transition. The district-level vertical team is composed of a school board member; the superintendent; an assistant superintendent; building principals from the high school, middle school, and elementary school levels; a teacher from each of these levels; and a college professor. In addition, educators in each school are designing their own vertical teams. Each team focuses on the goal of collaborative planning of school improvement.

Inner-City Planning

Even that quintessential inner-city school district, New York City, has begun to examine ways in which the principles of school organization, developing at the middle level, can be applied to the high school. Educators at a group of alternative high schools have been exploring ways in which their large, factory-style schools might become smaller, more intimate communities for learning. As a result of historic agreements between the Board and the United Federation of Teachers to implement shared decision making, teachers and administrators have been investigating models of collaborative planning and the development of "cluster models." Such models incorporate flexible scheduling and grouping of students, common planning time, team teaching, and thematic approaches to the curriculum. Faculty members in some secondary schools in New York City have designed organizational plans that will permit them to teach the same students for three years, making for truly long-term teacher-student relationships.

Interdisciplinary Connections in High School

Similar activity, with an interdisciplinary emphasis, is occurring in other districts. At Nevada Union High School, in Grass Valley, California, the 9th grade has been organized into an interdisciplinary team format. The program combines the study of world history and English, and that of mathematics and science, into two double-period blocks, much like those of middle schools. According to Principal Larry Meek (personal communication, April 1989), the goal of the program is to stress connections between academic disciplines and to promote more opportunity for increased teacher-student bonding and adjustment to individual differences. Arguing that the transition from the middle level to the high school can be disorienting, Meek says that the two-hour blocks of time do allow for the establishment of quality relationships between teacher and student, and among students. The program, says Meek, has reduced the number of attendance and discipline problems.

We believe that these activities demonstrate the power of the interdisciplinary component of the middle school model for its own students and its obvious attractive applicability at the high school, as well. Our prediction is that, by the end of the century, hundreds of American high schools will have been reorganized into an interdisciplinary approach at the 9th grade. It is possible that such an interdisciplinary approach at the high school level will not stop at the 9th grade. Indeed, a number of high schools have already established pilot programs in the senior high school years.

■ At Amityville Memorial High School in Amityville, New York, an interdisciplinary curriculum involves students in grades 11 and 12. A comprehensive integration of American history and literature through the reading of historical novels, poems, essays, and autobiographies, the course aims at the development, simultaneously, of a critical perspective and an historical viewpoint. The course is taught by a team of teachers from the history and English departments.

■ High schools in Tucson, Arizona, are exploring new horizons in interdisciplinary approaches. At Amphitheater High School, a team of three teachers of 11th graders join three courses: U.S. history, U.S. literature, and conceptual physics. Principal Mary J. Monroe says that course content is planned along thematic lines with projects in each class consistent with the theme. At Catalina High School, also in Tucson, interdisciplinary team organization has been facilitated by having the number of department chair positions cut in half (Cawelti 1989).

■ Six teachers comprise an interdisciplinary team at American High School in Fremont, California. These teachers plan and teach a two-year (10th and 11th grade) program in American history and literature to 180 students. Principal Joe Tranchia reports that students enrolled in this program have consistently scored in higher percentage rankings than students who take the courses in separate entities. We would predict other positive outcomes as well.

■ At Edsel Ford High School in Dearborn, Michigan, a team of teachers are responsible for a three-year interdisciplinary program for students identified as "at risk" in the 9th grade. Students volunteer for Providing Alternatives Choices in Education (PACE). The purpose of the program, according to Principal Robert Young, is to create a climate in which self-concept and academic standing are improved and to enable the at-risk student to successfully complete high school. Two academic teachers work together, with a support staff of art and music teachers, counselors, and administrators.

Funding for Teaming

In 1989, the school board at Phoenix Union High School District in Phoenix, Arizona, invested $2.1 million to establish interdisciplinary teams at the South Mountain High School. Aimed at improving academic achievement and increasing the enrollment of white students, the money was spent to increase the number of teachers so that they could be organized into teams and have the planning time they needed to work together effectively. The hope was that this would improve instruction, raise student achievement, and cause the school's reputation to soar, and that white students, who had been leaving the school for other options, would come just to take advantage of the program (Needham 1989).

Dramatically increased planning time permits close student contact, parent contact, even close colleague contact. The key to the effects of the program on students is what teachers at South Mountain call "coring," a version of the interdisciplinary team organization. Students move from one subject to another as a core-group class. Freshmen are grouped for mathematics, science, and English; sophomores for social studies and English. The result is interdisciplinary teams of teachers who share the same students, the same part of the building, the same schedule, and the responsibility for planning major portions of the students' academic program.

Teachers at South Mountain call it "massive omniscience" (Needham 1989). Teachers collaborate with each other in supervising students and in letting the students know that the teachers know and care about them. Time to plan together leads quite naturally to attempts to design joint interdisciplinary projects that make classes more interesting. The results seem quite positive. The dropout rate has declined in one year from 22.8 to 17.3 percent. Departments, finding their students more successful, are phasing out easy courses like basic mathematics; and teachers are hoping to reach the point where every student will take Algebra I instead. The school librarian reports that students are doing more research there on more interesting topics. Teachers are more enthusiastic about their work than before the teaming.

Comprehensive Innovations

Andrew High School, in Tinley Park, Illinois, has 2,100 students and 135 teachers. Its principal, Tim Brown (personal communication, March 1989), describes a veritable whirlwind of interdisciplinary and other innovative efforts emerging from values and concepts similar to those found in the most effective middle schools.

■ A 9th grade interdisciplinary humanities program involves sixty students in a heterogeneously grouped, thematic approach to contemporary cultures. Four teachers (English, social studies, music, and art) share the same students, the same room (which is large and flexible), and the same schedule for two and one-half hours each day. Using common planning time and block scheduling, similar to that of middle schools, the teachers provide a program that yields three credits to participating students (1 credit in English, 1 credit in art, ½ credit in social studies, and ½ credit in music). Teachers in the program teach two other classes each during the school day. Brown says that the program is popular; fully enrolled on a first-come, first-served basis; and open to all students regardless of whether they are otherwise enrolled in honors or basic classes during other parts of their day.

■ A 10th grade innovation is underway—an interdisciplinary geometry course. Three teachers (mathematics, art, and applied technology) team together to teach standard geometry concepts through the use of art and technology. The teachers make an effort to be truly interdisciplinary, so that students are unable to determine which one is the "real" math teacher. So far the effort has been successful. The teachers think of themselves as teachers of interdisciplinary geometry.

■ During the 1990-91 school year, an interdisciplinary food science program was launched. The course runs for two hours each day, involving both home economics and physical education teachers, with the assistance of a science teacher. Students earn one credit for physical education and one credit for home economics. It aims at real team teaching, not turn teaching, says Brown. The focus is on nutrition and involves, in particular, students who have nutrition problems in their personal lives. Students in the program have physical education together and eat lunch as a team.

■ Anxious about tracking and its effects on basic-level students, staff members have implemented a program including what they call an "academic homeroom." So-called "basic" students join a regular academic class for sixty minutes, then they join the academic homeroom for thirty minutes. The purpose of the academic homeroom is to give the students the extra help they need to stay in place in the science, mathematics, and English courses they may be taking. According to Brown, the grades of many of these students have improved to a B level.

■ A Peer Helpers program, in its fourth year. has grown to be a critical dimension of Andrew High School. At the beginning of the year, the staff conducts a sociogram in which they ask the high school students to identify the thirty most facilitative peers, those to whom they would go for help with a problem. The identified students are invited to complete training in peer facilitation, enabling them to listen more effectively and to be able to refer students with needs to more professional resources.

■ A 9th grade advisory program, which will go beyond orientation, is being planned. Every teacher in the school will take responsibility for four 9th graders for a day of orientation at the beginning of the school year. Then these adults will retain advisory responsibilities for the students for the remainder of the year. At this point, the staff is thinking that they may hang on to these four students and add four more at the beginning of the next year. The aim is, in part, what Brown calls "intensive acclimation" in a very short time. "We want to make sure, from day one, that these students know there is a caring adult in the building, who is interested in looking after them."

Interdisciplinary Empowerment at a New School

Florin High School, near Sacramento, has been organized in an astonishingly interdisciplinary manner, as described earlier in this chapter. Influenced by participation in an ASCD High School Futures Consortium, the staff has arranged the faculty into four (soon to be five) inter-disciplinary divisions, which the principal, William Huyett (personal communication, 1989), describes as "a kind of core approach" where the students stay together, but the teachers rotate.

As in other interdisciplinary programs described in this chapter, Florin High School teachers who are members of teaching teams share the same students, the same part of the building, the same lunchtime, and the same planning periods. Teachers on these teams are empowered to make many decisions, especially regarding the curriculum. Because there are no textbooks in the program, teachers develop the curriculum together.

It is important to note that, unlike many other high school interdis-ciplinary efforts, the Florin program is for all students in the school (currently grades 9-10), not just a special group, and will eventually develop into an interdisciplinary team approach for all students in grades 9-12. Perhaps even more avant garde, in our view, is the plan to move to a more and more heterogeneously grouped organization of students. Currently, each area offers one honors section only, with the remainder being standard groups of students. William Huyett dreams of someday doing away with all tracking and ability grouping in the school but recognizes that the community, in particular, is not ready for that.

Humanities Without Tracking

In wealthy, suburban Sandy Hook, Connecticut, staff members at New-town High School are moving in similar directions. Principal Bill Man-fredonia is ebullient about the humanities program there and the poten-tial it offers for moving into a real school-within-a-school program, with truly interdisciplinary teaching. The program at Newtown High features teachers on teams with adjoining rooms and with similar blocks of plan-ning time. The program is offered to all students, without tracking of any kind.

Manfredonia (personal communication, Spring 1989) says his faculty wants real interdisciplinary teaching, too—not just turn teaching, in which the English teacher comes in and teaches English. At Newtown, the staff is trying to get a waiver on the Carnegie unit, to facilitate even more flexibility.

■   ■   ■

Without taking away from the excitement of the efforts described here, all are at least familiar to educators experienced in the implementation of interdisciplinary team and advisory programs at the middle level. Creating smallness within bigness, as well as acknowledging the needs of a particular age group, to achieve a more positive structure remains the hallmark of the modern middle school movement. But, as we have seen, these structures are appearing in other schools, as well.

We think these programs illustrate a major event in schooling. Such programs, with a curriculum scope and sequence developed from the early elementary years, through the middle school, and on to the high school, may offer an unusual opportunity to weave a truly common, new thread into the current fabric of the K-12 curriculum. We may be witness to a bright new color in the educational rainbow.

Beyond to Our Future

In 1990, the National Middle School Association (NMSA) conducted a study of educators' opinions about the future of middle school education, using what is known as the Delphi technique. Delphi forecasting is a technique used to systematically develop expert opinion and consensus about the future. This technique, in essence, pools individual opinion about issues and events in a given area to develop forecasts that are likely to be more accurate than any one individual's opinion (Dull 1988). As a short-term forecasting tool, the process requires a panel of experts in a given field to determine the most significant changes to occur in that field in terms of events and issues. The panel then sets the time frame within which the events are most likely to occur, the probability of the changes, the desirability of the changes, and selected elements that will help or hinder the changes. Throughout all the rounds (of which, in the NMSA study, there were four), the panel works on a mandatory consensus model, responding to all items from the last consensus round.

In the NMSA study, the questions asked of the Delphi panel concerned what issues or events in middle-level education would affect the profession in the next twenty years. From several hundred initial responses, the consensus technique and a cross-impact matrix analysis resulted in thirty-four top priorities. NMSA's purpose was to use the consensus information to help set a global agenda and to develop a strategic plan for the organization itself, as well as for middle-level education more generally. Further, the Delphi results could help various groups of people establish priorities, allocate resources and personnel, and promote and foster research initiatives. In essence, the results were to be added to the existing research database to help middle-level educators be even more proactive in their efforts. What the Delphi revealed essentially supports much of what has been discussed and illustrated throughout this book.

Panel members agreed on the importance not only of building but sustaining the middle school concept as the most desirable educational model for young adolescents. Many of the experts had served in middle schools for a number of years, and they were well aware of the problems associated with keeping a school true to its goals and philosophy after the glow of transition and the early years had passed. They listed issues surrounding leadership and the necessity for having a well-articulated philosophy and a vision for what the schools were to be three, five, or even ten years after the initial opening.

Not only did the study affirm the middle school concept, it recognized the need to promote middle schools as a legitimate third tier of American education. Panel members spoke of their concerns that although there is a common vocabulary for both elementary and secondary levels, too few people are aware of the issues and concerns specific to the middle school. Some of the issues they suggested related to having enhanced programs for learners with specific needs in the middle school. Echoing the intent of the Carnegie Task Force report, the panel gave a high priority to issues of health education, programs for at-risk students, and programs related to substance use and abuse.

The panel of experts spoke in one voice about the essential issue of middle grades teacher preparation and certification. Almost every respondent listed the necessity for teachers to be specifically prepared or recertified for teaching at the middle level. They spoke about the need for state departments of education and institutions of higher learning to lead this effort. They were eloquent in their beliefs that this cadre of specifically prepared teachers was quite likely the key to the movement's success or failure.

Middle level teachers must have a thorough knowledge of young adolescent characteristics. This knowledge, plus an acceptance of the normal behavior of 10- to 14-year-olds, could result in curriculum changes—making studies more relevant and meaningful to the student. The panel also indicated that this knowledge could result in instruction more mindful of the behavioral characteristics and normal patterns of young adolescent learning. These have been two of the major premises of this book and a conviction with which we obviously agree.

The term *beyond*, in the case of this book, has two implications. One is that practices found to be successful in the middle school are now being used in elementary and high schools with significantly positive results. Second, there is growing evidence, from studies such as the Delphi, that we have been correct in insisting that we do, indeed, know a more effective way to go about educating young adolescents for the new century . . . and beyond.

■   ■   ■

When Doris Jenkins, chair of the department of curriculum and instruction at Appalachia State University, agreed to conduct a Delphi Project for the National Middle School Association, she admitted to a certain degree of naivete about the magnitude of the study. After eight months, hundreds of hours of computer time, reams of paper, and too many pink message slips to count, she was, by her own admission, tired but wiser.

She says that working with the project reminded her of how people can become dedicated to a task they view as valuable, one in which their input is genuinely meaningful. Panel members evidently were quite interested in the project, she says, because almost 80 percent (rather than the expected 15-20 percent) responded to the initial round of questions. Even more gratifying, they continued to participate through all four arduous rounds of the project.

Jenkins says she was impressed with the depth of thought the panel put into their responses as well as their considerable breadth of knowledge about middle level education. She was surprised and a little amused, however, at the abbreviated time frame for events and issues proposed by the panel. Given that they were asked to predict events and issues that would happen in middle school education in the next twenty years, the Delphi panel predicted that almost all the events would happen in just five years. She laughingly told us that, in many cases, these people have been waiting for thirty years—and they just aren't willing to wait patiently much longer. In their opinion, the place is here and the time is now.

References

Adams, C. (1989). "The Teacher Journal: A Better Way to Show Your Success." *Learning* 18, 3: 57-59.

Aiken, W. (1941). *The Story of The Eight Year Study*. New York: Harper and Row.

Alberty, H., and E. Alberty. (1962). *Reorganizing the High School Curriculum*. Rev. ed. New York: Macmillan.

Alexander, W.M., and P.S. George. (1981). *The Exemplary Middle School*. New York: Holt, Rinehart & Winston.

Alexander, W., and C.K. McEwin. (1989a). *Earmarks of Schools in the Middle: A Research Report*. Boone, N.C.: Appalachian State University.

Alexander, W., and C.K. McEwin. (1989b). *Schools in the Middle: Status and Progress*. Columbus, Ohio: National Middle School Association.

Alexander, W., and E. Williams. (December 1965). "Schools in The Middle Years." *Educational Leadership* 23, 3: 217-223.

Alexander, W., E. Williams, M. Compton, V. Hines, and D. Prescott. (1968). *The Emergent Middle School*. New York: Holt, Rinehart and Winston.

Ames, L.B., F.I. Ilg, and S.M. Baker. (1988). *Your Ten-to-Fourteen-Year-Old*. New York: Delacorte.

Andrus, E., and D. Joiner. (May 1989). "The Community Needs H.U.G.S.S. Too!" *Middle School Journal* 20, 5: 8-11.

Apple, M. (1986). *Teachers and Texts*. Boston and London: Routledge & Kegan Paul.

Arnold, J. (May 1985). "A Responsive Curriculum for Emerging Adolescents." *Middle School Journal* 16: 3, 14-18.

ASCD. (1975). *The Middle School We Need*. Washington, D.C.: Association for Supervision and Curriculum Development.

ASCD Curriculum Update. September 1990.

Barnhart, E. (1987). "Providing Appropriate Exploratory Programs for Students in the Middle Grades." *ERS Spectrum* 5: 15-19.

Beane, J. (Summer 1975). "The Case for Core in the Middle School." *Middle School Journal* 6: 33-4.

Beane, J. (January 1980). "The General Education We Need." *Educational Leadership* 37, 4: 307-308.

Beane, J. (1987). "Dance to the Music of Time: The Future of Middle Level Education." *NASSP—Schools in the Middle* newsletter, 1-8.

Beane, J. (May 1990a). "Rethinking the Middle School Curriculum." *Middle School Journal* 21: 1-5.

Beane, J. (1990b). *A Middle School Curriculum: From Rhetoric to Reality*. Columbus, Ohio: National Middle School Association.

Beane, J. (1990c). *Affect in the Curriculum: Toward Democracy, Dignity, and Diversity*. New York: Teachers College Press.

Beane, J., and R. Lipka. (1986). *Self-Concept, Self-Esteem, and the Curriculum*. New York: Teachers College Press.

Beane, J., and R. Lipka. (1987). *When the Kids Come First: Enhancing Self-Esteem*. Columbus, Ohio: National Middle School Association.

Benson, P.L., D.L. Williams, and A.L. Johnson. (1987). *The Quicksilver Years: The Hopes and Fears of Early Adolescence.* San Francisco: Harper and Row.

Bolton, R. (1979). *People Skills.* Englewood Cliffs, N.J.: Prentice-Hall, Inc.

Brazee, E. (1989). "The Tip of the Iceberg or the Edge of the Glacier: Curriculum Development in Middle School." *Mainely Middle* 1: 18-22.

Brown, J.G., and A.W. Howard. (January 1972). "Who Should Teach at Schools for the Middle Years?" *The Clearing House* 46: 279-283.

Carnegie Council on Adolescent Development. (1989). *Turning Points: Preparing Youth for the 21st Century.* New York: Carnegie Corporation.

Carr, J.F. (1989). "By Chance and Connection, There by Choice: Teachers Who Like to Teach in the Middle Grades." Unpublished doctoral dissertation. Burlington: University of Vermont.

Carr, J., P. Eppig, and P. Monether. (February 1986). "Learning by Solving Real Problems." *Middle School Journal* 17, 2: 14-16.

Case, A. (May 1989). "A Comprehensive Orientation Program for Incoming Sixth Graders." *Middle School Journal* 20, 5: 26-28.

Cawelti, G. (November 1988). "Middle Schools a Better Match with Early Adolescent Needs, ASCD Survey Finds." *ASCD Curriculum Update*, pp. 1-12.

Cawelti, G. (April 1989). "Designing High Schools for the Future." *Educational Leadership* 47, 7: 30-35.

Clark, S.N., and D.C. Clark.(1987). "Interdisciplinary Teaching Programs: Organization, Rationale, and Implementation." *NASSP Bulletin* 71: 1-6.

Collamore, J. A. Pierce, and L. Davis. (September 1988). "A Medieval Fair Brought History Alive." *Middle School Journal* 20, 1: 39-40.

Combs, A. (February 1957). "The Myth of Competition." *Childhood Education* 33: 264-68.

Commission on Secondary Curriculum. (1961). *The Junior High School We Need.* Washington D.C.: Association for Supervision and Curriculum Development.

Connors, N.A., and J.L. Irvin. (May 1989). "Is 'Middle-Schoolness' an Indicator of Excellence?" *Middle School Journal* 20, 5: 12-14.

Council on the Emerging Adolescent Learner. (1975). "The Middle School We Need." Washington, D.C.: Association for Supervision and Curriculum Development.

Crabbe, A.B. (September 1989). "The Future Problem Solving Program." *Educational Leadership* 47, 1: 27-29.

Cross Keys Middle School. (1990). *A Place of Our Own.* Florrisant, Mo.: Ferguson-Florrisant Public Schools.

Dawson, J. (1987). "Helping At-Risk Students in Middle Schools." *NASSP Bulletin* 71: 84-88.

Delaney, J.D. (1986). "Developing a Middle School Homeroom Guidance Program." *NASSP Bulletin* 70: 96-98.

Derrico, P.J. (April 1988). "Learning to Think with Philosophy for Children." *Educational Leadership* 45, 7: 34.

Dewey, J. (1902). *The Child and the Curriculum.* Chicago: University of Chicago Press.

Dickinson, T.S. (November 1988). "Small Stories." *Middle School Journal* 20: 12-13.

Dickson, D., and T. Knarr. (1989). *The School Improvement Process: An Explanation of the History and Concept of this Process in Hammond.* Hammond, Ind.: Hammond Public Schools.

Dixon, Nancy M. (November 1985). "The Implementation of Learning Style Information." *Lifelong Learning* 9,3: 16-18, 26.

Doda, N., P. George, and K. McEwin. (May 1987). "Ten Current Truths About Effective Schools." *Middle School Journal* 18, 3: 3-5.

Dryfoos, J. (January 1990). "The Achievement Train: Can High-Risk Children Get on Board?" *The Harvard Education Letter,* pp. 1-4.

Dull, R. (1988). "Delphi Forecasting: Market Research Method of the 1990s." *Marketing News* 22, 17: 143-147.

Eichorn, D.H. (1966). *The Middle School.* New York: The Center for Applied Research.

Elkind, D. (1984). *All Grown Up and No Place To Go: Teenagers in Crisis.* Reading, Mass.: Addison Wesley.

Epstein, J.L. (1990). "What Matters in the Middle Grades—Grade Span or Practices?" *Phi Delta Kappan* 71, 6: 438-444.

Erb, T.O., and N.M. Doda. (1989). *Team Organization: Promises and Possibilities* (Action series). Washington, D.C.: National Education Association.

Erikson, E.H. (1986). *Childhood and Society.* New York: Norton.

Erikson, E.H. (1968). *Youth, Identity, and Crisis.* New York: Norton.

Faunce, R., and N. Bossing. (1951). *Developing the Core Curriculum.* New York: Prentice-Hall.

Florida State Department of Education. (1986). *Florida's Teachers as Advisor Program: Guide for Implementation.* Tallahassee: Florida State Department of Education.

Gabel, C. (November 1985). "Exploratory Activities—Adapting to the '80s." *Middle School Journal* 17, 1: 22-24.

Gardner, D. (April, 1983). *A Nation at Risk: The Imperative for Educational Reform. An Open Letter to the American People.* A Report to the Nation and the Secretary of Education. Washington, D.C.: National Commission on Excellence in Education.

Gardner, H. (1989). "Balancing Specialized and Comprehensive Knowledge." In *Schooling for Tomorrow,* edited by T. J. Sergiovanni and J. H. Moore. Boston: Allyn & Bacon.

Garvin, J.P. (1987). "Beliefs That Make a Difference." *Educational Oasis* 7: 7.

Garvin, J.P. (November 1987). "What Do Parents Expect from Middle Level Schools?" *Middle School Journal* 19, 1: 3-4.

George, P.S. (1975). *Ten Years of Open Space Schools: A Review of the Research.* Gainesville: Florida Educational Research and Development Council.

George, P.S. (1982). "Interdisciplinary Team Organization: Four Operational Phases." *Middle School Journal* 14: 10-13.

George, P.S. (1983). *The Theory Z School: Beyond Effectiveness.* Columbus, Ohio: National Middle School Association.

George, P.S. (1987). "Team Building Without Tears." *Personnel Journal* 66: 122-129.

George, P.S. (September 1988). "Tracking and Ability Grouping: Which Way For the Middle School?" *Middle School Journal* 20: 21-28.

George, P.S. (1989). "Maintaining the Middle School: A National Survey." *NASSP Bulletin* 73, 521: 67-74.

George, P.S. (February 1990a). "From Junior High to Middle School—Principals' Perspectives." *NASSP Bulletin* 74, 523: 86-94.

George, P.S. (1990b). "Middle School Principals." Unpublished raw data.

George, P.S., and W.G. Anderson. (1989). "Maintaining the Middle School: A National Survey." *NASSP Bulletin* 73, 521: 67-74.

George, P.S., E. George, and T. Abiko. (1989). *The Japanese Junior High School: A View From the Inside.* Columbus, Ohio: National Middle School Association.

George, P.S., L. Oldaker. (1985a). *Evidence for the Middle School.* Columbus, Ohio: National Middle School Association.

George, P.S., L. Oldaker. (December 1985b). "A National Survey of Middle School Effectiveness." *Educational Leadership* 43, 4: 79-85.

George, P.S., M. Spreul, and J. Moorefield. (1986). *Long-Term Teacher/Student Relationships: A Middle School Case Study.* Columbus, Ohio: National Middle School Association.

George, P.S., C. Stevenson. (1989). "The 'Very Best Teams' in the 'Best Schools' as Described by Middle School Principals." *TEAM* 3: 6-14.

Gibbs, N. (January 1989). "For Goodness' Sake." *Time*, pp. 20-24.

Glant, L. (January 1989). "Moving to the Middle Without Misery." *Middle School Journal* 20, 3: 12-14.

Glickman, C. (1985). *Developmental Supervision.* Boston: Allyn & Bacon.

Goodlad, J.I. (1984). *A Place Called School: Prospects for the Future.* New York: McGraw-Hill.

Gordon, T. (1977). *Leadership Effectiveness Training.* New York: Bantam Books.

Grantes, J., C. Noyce, F. Patterson, and J. Robertson. (1961). *The Junior High School We Need.* Washington, D.C.: Association for Supervision and Curriculum Development.

Grooms, M.A. (1967). *Perspectives on the Middle School.* Columbus, Ohio: Charles E. Merrill.

Gruhn, W., and H. Douglass. (1947). *The Modern Junior High School.* New York: Ronald.

Gruhn, W., and H. Douglas. (1971). *The Modern Junior High School.* 3d ed. New York: The Ronald Press.

Hall, G.S. (1904). *Adolescence.* New York: Appleton-Century-Crofts.

Hanus, K.S. (November 1987). "Jeremy: An LD Student Teaches the Teacher." *Middle School Journal* 19, 1: 31.

Hargreaves, A. (1986). *Two Cultures of Schooling: The Case of Middle Schools.* London: Falmer.

Hart, G. (November 1989) "Educational Value—A Response to the Question 'Just What Should Every Early Adolescent Know?'" *Middle School Journal* 21, 2: 29.

Havighurst, R. (1953). *Developmental Tasks and Education.* New York: McKay.

Hock, L., and T. Hill. (1960). *The General Education Class in the Secondary School*. New York: Holt-Rinehart.

Hopkins, L.T. (1941). *Interaction: The Democratic Process*. New York: D.C. Heath.

Hopkins, L.T. (1955). *The Core Program: Integration and Interaction*. New York: Board of Education of the City of New York.

Howard, A., and G. Stoumbis. (1970). *The Junior High and Middle School: Issues and Practicss*. Toronto: Intext Educational Publishers.

Howe, S.F. (1989). "Rubbing Elbows with Reality." *Learning* 18, 3: 48-50, 52.

Inhelder, B., and J. Piaget. (1958). *The Growth of Logical Thinking From Childhood to Adolescence*. New York: Basic Books.

Jacobs, H.H., ed. (1989). *Interdisciplinary Curriculum: Design and Implementation*. Alexandria, Va.: Association for Supervision and Curriculum Development.

James, C. (1972). *Young Lives at Stake*. New York: Agathon.

James, C. (1974). *Beyond Customs: An Educator's Journey*. New York: Agathon.

James, M. (1986). *Advisor-Advisee Programs: Why, What and How*. Columbus, Ohio: National Middle School Association.

Jenkins, J., ed. (1988). *Teachers as Advisors Program: Evaluation Report*. Tallahassee: Florida State Department of Education.

Johnson, D.W., and R.T. Johnson. (December 1989). "Social Skills for Successful Group Work." *Educational Leadership* 47, 4: 29.33.

Johnson, D.W., R.T. Johnson, and E.J. Holubec. (1988). *Cooperation in the Classroom*. Edina, Minn.: Interaction Book Company.

Kagan, S. (December 1989). "The Structural Approach to Cooperative Learning." *Educational Leadership* 47, 4: 12-15.

Kammeraad-Campbell, S. (1989). *Doc: The Story of Dennis Littky and His Fight for a Better School*. Chicago: Contemporary Books.

Keefe, James W. (1986). "Advisement Programs—Improving Teacher-Student Relationships." *NASSP Bulletin* 70, 489: 85-90.

Kennedy, P. (1988). *The Rise and Fall of the Great Powers*. New York: Macmillan.

Kierstead, J., and S. Mentor. (October 1988). "Translating the Vision Into Reality in California Schools." *Educational Leadership* 46, 2: 35-40.

Kliebard, H. (1986). *The Struggle for the American Curriculum: 1893-1958*. Boston and London: Routledge & Kegan Paul.

Krumbein, G. (1989). "Student Leadership Groups at the Middle Level." *NASSP Bulletin* 73, 516: 40-44.

Landfried, S.E. (May 1988). "Talking to Kids About Things that Matter." *Educational Leadership* 45, 8: 32-35.

Lawton, E.J. (1987). "True Middle Level Education—Keeping Student Characteristics in Mind." *NASSP Bulletin* 71, 502: 115-120.

Lewis, A.C. (1988). *Facts and Faith: A Status Report on Youth Service*. Washington, D.C.: William T. Grant Foundation.

Lipka, R.P. (1989). "Teachers as Students: Implications for Student Self-Concept and Self-Esteem." *NELMS Journal* 2: 6-7.

Lipsitz, J. (1984). *Successful Schools for Young Adolescents*. New Brunswick, N.J.: Transaction.

Lounsbury, J. (December 1960). "How the Junior High School Came to Be." *Educational Leadership* 18, 3: 145-147.

Lounsbury, J. (July 1988). "1988 National Teacher of the Year. *Middle School Journal* 19, 4: 3-4.

Lounsbury, J. (January 1989). "Just What Should Every Early Adolescent Know?" *Middle School Journal* 20, 3: 39.

Lounsbury, J., and G. Vars. (1978). *A Curriculum for the Middle School Years.* Columbus, Ohio: Charles E. Merrill.

Lurry, L., and E. Alberty. (1957). *Developing a High School Core Program.* New York: Macmillan.

MacIver, D. (1990). "Meeting the Needs of Young Adolescents: Advisory Groups, Interdisciplinary Teaching Teams, and School Transition Programs." *Phi Delta Kappan* 71, 6: 458-464.

Maeroff, G. (1988). "Withered Hopes, Stillborn Dreams: The Dismal Panorama of Urban Schools." *Phi Delta Kappan* 69, 9: 632-638.

Manning, M.L. (1988). "Erikson's Psychological Theories Help Explain Early Adolescence." *NASSP Bulletin* 72, 509: 95-101.

Marshall, J. (1986). *Dealing with Difficult Behavior.* New York: American Management Association.

McDonough, L. (1991). "Middle Level Curriculum: The Search for Self and Social Meaning." *Middle School Journal* 23: 29-35.

McWalters, P. (1989). *Superintendent's Proposal to the Board of Education. Position Paper on the Redesign of Public Education in Rochester.* Rochester, N.Y.: Rochester City School District.

Melchior, T.M., R.E. Kaufold, and E. Edwards. (April 1988). "Using CoRT Thinking in Schools" *Educational Leadership* 45, 7: 32-33.

Messina, A. (1989). "The Classroom Computer Music Workstation of the Future." *NELMS Journal* 2: 8-9.

Mickelson, J. (1957). "What Does Research Say About the Effectivenessof the Core Curriculum." *School Review* 65: 144-60.

Middle Grade Task Force. (1987). *Caught in the Middle: The Task of Educational Reform for Young Adolescents in California Schools.* Sacramento: California State Department of Public Instruction.

Mohr, P.H., N.A. Sprinthall, and E.R. Gerler, Jr. (November 1987). "Moral Reasoning in Early Adolescence: Implications for Drug Abuse Prevention." *The School Counselor* 35, 2: 120-127.

Moore, M.L. (1989). *Sarasota Middle School.* Sarasota, Fla.: Sarasota County School Board.

Morgan, L. (1987). *Freeport High School Advisor Handbook.* Freeport, Fla.: School Board of Walton County.

Moss, T. (1969). *Middle School.* New York: Houghton Mifflin.

Myrick, R.D., M. Highland, and B. Highland. (1986). "Preparing Teachers to Be Advisors." *Middle School Notes,* 44-45.

National Association of Secondary School Principals. (1985). *An Agenda for Excellence at the Middle Level.* Reston, Va.: National Association of Secondary School Principals.

Needham, N. (1989). "We've Got the Time to Teach." *NEA Today,* 4-5.

NMSA Resolutions Committee. (January 1989). "National Middle School Association 1988-89 Resolutions." *Middle School Journal* 20, 3: 18-20.

North Carolina State Department of Education. (1985). *Effective Teacher Training Program*. Raleigh: North Carolina State Department of Education.

Peters, T.J., and R.H. Waterman, Jr. (1982). *In Search of Excellence: Lessons from America's Best-Run Companies*. New York: Harper.

Piaget, J. (1973). *The Child and Reality*. New York: Grossman.

Plodzik, K.T., and P. George. (May 1989). "Interdisciplinary Team Organization." *Middle School Journal* 20, 5: 15-17.

Pokewitz, T., ed. (1987). *The Formation of School Subjects: The Struggle for Creating an American Institution*. New York: Falmer.

Putbrese, L. (February 1989). "Advisory Programs at the Middle Level—The Students' Response." *NASSP Bulletin* 73, 514: 111-115.

Reck, R., and B. Long. (1985). *The Win-Win Negotiator*. Escondido, Calif.: Blanchard Training and Development, Inc.

Rhodes, R., and F. Strong. (February 1989). "Hey, Teacher, May I Please Take My Test?" *Middle School Journal* 21, 1: 44-45.

Rochester City School District. (1988). *Guidelines for School-Based Planning*. Rochester, N.Y.: Rochester City School District.

Rosenshine, B.V. (1979). "Content, Time, and Direct Instruction." In *Research on Teaching: Concepts, Findings, and Implications*, edited by P. Peterson and J. Herbert. Berkeley: McCutchan Publishing Company.

Rugg, H., and A. Shumaker. (1928). *The Child-Centered School*. New York: World Book.

Saterlie, M.E. (May 1988). "Developing a Community Consensus for Teaching Values." *Educational Leadership* 45, 8: 44-47.

Schwartz, L.J., and F. Corvasce. (May 1987). "The Buddy Program: A Peer-Affective Educational Program in the Middle School." *Middle School Journal* 18, 3: 27-29.

Silberman, C. (1970). *Crisis in the Classroom*. New York: Random House.

Slavin, R.E. (1987). "Ability Grouping and Student Achievement in Elementary Schools: A Best Evidence Synthesis." *Review of Educational Research* 57, 3: 293-336.

Smith, B., W. Stanley, and J.H. Shores. (1950). *Fundamentals of Curriculum Development*. New York: Harcourt, Brace & World.

Southern Association of College and Secondary Schools. (1958). *The Junior High School Program*. Atlanta, Ga.: The Association of College and Secondary Schools.

Speaker's Task Force. (1984). *The Forgotten Years: Report of the Speaker's Task Force on Middle Childhood Education*. Tallahassee: Florida House of Representatives.

Spindler, J., and P. George. (March 1984). "Participatory Leadership in the Middle School." *The Clearing House* 57, 7: 293-295.

Stanfield, H. (January 1990). "In This Corner of the World, the Children are Secure and I Helped to Make It So." *Middle School Journal* 21, 3: 45.

Sterrett-Pegg, J. (March 1989). "Just What Should Every Early Adolescent Know—A Reader Reflects." *Middle School Journal* 20, 4: 37.

Stevenson, C. (1986). *Teachers as Inquirers: Strategies for Learning With and About Early Adolescents*. Columbus, Ohio: National Middle School Association.

Stevenson, C., and J.F. Carr. (In press). *Integrated Studies in the Middle Grades: Dancing Through Walls*. New York: Teachers College Press.

Strubbe, M.A. (January 1990). "Are Interdisciplinary Units Worthwhile? Ask Students!" *Middle School Journal* 21, 3: 36-38.

Tanner, D., and L. Tanner. (1980). *Curriculum Development: Theory Into Practice*. New York: Macmillan.

Thomason, J. (August 1984). "Nurturing the Nature of Early Adolescents—Or a Day at the Zoo." *Middle School Journal* 15, 4: 3-6.

Thomason, J. (1989). "Don't Early Adolescents Ever Fit?" *Transescence: The Journal on Emerging Adolescent Education* 17: 15-19.

Timmer, N. (1977). "An Investigation into the Degree of Understanding of the Developmental Characteristics of Pre- and Early Adolescents by Junior High and Middle Level School Teachers." *Dissertation Abstracts International* 38: 03A. (University Microfilms No. DA598133.)

Toepfer, C. (February 1962). "Historical Development of Curricular Patterns of Junior High School Organization in America." *NASSP Bulletin* 46, 271: 181-183.

Tye, K. (1985). *The Junior High: School in Search of a Mission*. New York: University Press of America.

Van Hoose, J.V., and D. Strahan. (1987). *Promoting Harmony in the Middle Grades: Meeting the Needs of Early Adolescents*. Greensboro, N.C.: North Carolina League of Middle Level Schools.

Van Til, W., G. Vars, and J. Lounsbury. (1961). *Modern Education for the Junior High School Years*. Indianapolis, Ind.: Bobbs-Merrill.

Vars, G. (January 1966). "Can Team Teaching Save the Core Curriculum?" *Phi Delta Kappan* 47, 5: 258-62.

Vars, G.F. (1987). *Interdisciplinary Teaching: Why and How*. Columbus, Ohio: National Middle School Association.

Wheelock, A., and G. Dorman. (1988). *Before It's Too Late: Dropout Prevention in the Middle Grades*. Carrboro, N.C.: Center for Early Adolescence; Boston: Massachusetts Advocacy Center.

Weisbord, M. (1987). *Productive Workplaces*. San Francisco: Jossey-Boss.

Wiedbusch, R.J., S. Tidrow-Nelson, and D. Johnson. (September 1989). "Smiles Across Miles." *Middle School Journal* 21, 1: 40-41.

Wigginton, E. (1976). *I Wished I'd Given My Son a Wild Raccoon*. New York: Anchor.

Wigginton, E. (1985). *Sometimes a Shining Moment: The Foxfire Experience*. New York: Anchor.

Worsham, A. (April 1988). "A 'Grow as You Go' Thinking Skills Model." *Educational Leadership* 45, 7: 56-57.

Wright, G. (1958). *Block-Time Classes and the Core Program*. Washington, D.C.: U.S. Government Printing Office.

Youngs, B.B. (February 1989). "The Phoenix Curriculum." *Educational Leadership* 46, 5: 24.

About the Authors

PAUL S. GEORGE is Professor of Education, Department of Educational Leadership, College of Education, University of Florida, 2403 Norman Hall, Gainesville, Florida 32611.

CHRIS STEVENSON is Associate Professor of Education, College of Education and Social Services, University of Vermont, Waterman 534 PECD, Burlington, Vermont 05405.

JULIA THOMASON is Professor, Department of Curriculum and Instruction, Appalachian State University, Boone, North Carolina 28608.

JAMES A. BEANE is Professor, National College of Education, National-Louis University, Granston, Illinois. He can be reached at 928 West Shore Drive, Madison, Wisconsin 53715.

Current ASCD Networks
for Middle School Educators

ASCD sponsors numerous networks that help members exchange ideas, share common interests, identify and solve problems, grow professionally, and establish collegial relationships. Four current networks may be of particular interest to readers of this book:

Middle Schools

Contact: Evelyn Maycumber, Middle Grades/Reading Consultant, Northeast Florida Educational Consortium, Rte. 1, Box 8500, Palatka, FL 32177. Telephone: (904) 329-3800. FAX: (904) 329-3835.

Student Empowerment for Lifelong Learning

Contact: Diane Cardinalli, 71781 San Gorgonio, Rancho Mirage, CA 92270. Telephone: (619) 346-8187.

Learning Community

Contact: F. James Clatworthy, School of Education, Oakland University, Rochester, MI 48309-4401. Telephone: (313) 370-3052. FAX: (313) 370-4202.

Interdisciplinary Curriculum

Contact: Benjamin F. Ebersole, Department of Education, University of Maryland, Baltimore County, Wilkens Avenue, Baltimore, MD 21228. Telephone: (301) 455-2378. FAX: (301) 455-3213.